DIVING I
MOZAMBIQUE

Robynn & Ross Hofmeyr

Published by Struik Travel & Heritage (an imprint of Penguin Random House South Africa (Pty) Ltd)
Reg. No. 1953/000441/07
The Estuaries No. 4, Oxbow Crescent (off Century Avenue), Century City, 7441, South Africa
PO Box 1144, Cape Town, 8000 South Africa

Visit www.penguinrandomhouse.co.za for updates, news, events and special offers.

First published in 2017 by Struik Travel & Heritage

10 9 8 7 6 5 4 3 2 1

Publisher: Pippa Parker
Managing editor: Helen de Villiers
Editor: Emily Donaldson
Designer: Gillian Black
Cartographer: Liezel Bohdanowicz

Reproduction by Resolution Colour (Pty) Ltd., Cape Town
Printed and bound by 1010 Printing International Ltd., China

Print: 9781775845256
Epub: 9781775845263
Epdf: 9781775845270

Front cover: Diver and whale shark (Claudia Pellarini, Bittenbysharks.com)
Back cover (left to right): Newly hatched turtle off Azura Quilalea (Claudia Pellarini, Azura Quilalea); Canyon dive site (Claudia Pellarini, Azura Quilalea); a diver photographs a smalleye stingray *Dasyatis microps* (Daniel van Duinkerken); blackspotted puffer *Arothron nigropunctatus* (Bozena Michalowski, Nuarro Lodge); Robynn Hofmeyr (Charles Martin Hallé)
Page 1: Diver and Indian Ocean bottlenose dolphin *Tursiops aduncus* (Simon de Waal)
Map and background images: Sand (Vitaly Korovin, Shutterstock.com); sea (Dudarev Mikhail, Shutterstock.com); notebook (My name is boy, Shutterstock.com)

> **The authors and publisher of this book accept no responsibility for any loss, injury or death sustained while using the book as a guide.**

ACKNOWLEDGEMENTS

We have had the privilege of diving with most of the resorts and dive centres included here and would like to thank everyone who has helped us in so many ways – from the logistics of getting from place to place, to giving us accommodation and taking us out on dives.

Our favourite fish reference book is Dennis King and Valda Fraser's *The Reef Guide*. We are so grateful to Dennis and Valda for offering to help us identify all the species in our book and for so willingly sharing their time, expertise and photographs.

We have to thank Claudia Pellarini, Dennis King, Smishyfish, Daniel van Duinkerken and the many other photographers for sharing their photographs with us. The book would be meaningless without the beauty you recorded.

Lastly, thank you to the team at Penguin Random House. To Pippa Parker who saw the possibilities, Gillian Black who did endless research, Liezel Bohdanowicz who created excellent maps and of course Emily Donaldson, who eased our way through every bump in the road with her calm demeanour and practical solutions.

Contents

Forewords 4
Preface 5
Introduction 6
Map of Mozambique 8

**Cabo Delgado Province &
The Quirimbas Archipelago 12**

'andBeyond' Vamizi Island
& Watersports Centre 16
Anantara Medjumbe Island Resort 18
Guludo Beach Lodge 26
Dive Quirimbas
at Ibo Island Lodge 28
Azura Quilalea Private Island 32
Situ Island Resort 40
CI Divers & Pieter's Place 44

Nampula Province 48

Nuarro Lodge 52
Kwalala Lodge &
Pelago Adventure Centre 56
Libélula 62

**Inhambane Province &
The Bazaruto Archipelago 66**

**Northern Inhambane &
The Bazaruto Archipelago 72**
Anantara Bazaruto Island Resort 74
Azura Benguerra 78
'andBeyond' Benguerra Island 80
Odyssea Dive 82
Dive Bazaruto 86

Southern Inhambane 88
Barra Reef Divers 90
Tofo Scuba 92
Diversity Scuba 98
Liquid Dive Adventures 100
Peri-Peri Divers 102
Marine Megafauna Foundation 105
Jeff's Palm Resort & Pro
Dive Centre 106
Guinjata Dive Centre 108
Paindane Dive Charter 112
Doxa Beach Hotel 115
Zavora Marine Lab 117
Zavora Lodge & Dive Centre 118
Wobbegong Dive Centre &
Nhanombe Lodge 122

Maputo Province 126
White Pearl Resorts 130
Back to Basics Adventures 132
Gozo Azul (Blue Fun) 135
Dolphin Encountours
Research Center 138
Scuba Adventures 140
The Whaler –
Underwater Explorer 142
Oceana Diving 146
Gala-Gala Eco Resort & Diving 148

Appendix – Health and safety 152

Forewords

Mozambique is a very special place, both on land and underwater. The warmth of the local people allied to a natural environment that – for me – celebrates the very essence of Africa, mean that it is a country that must be on any traveller's bucket list. Despite an increasingly well-established tourist infrastructure, there is still a sense of the pioneering spirit for anyone who travels within Mozambique, and this is never more applicable than when diving. The breadth of the undersea riches here is only really just coming to light, with exquisite reefs bathed in the warm waters of the Agulhas Current, and some world-class big animal encounters. Robynn and Ross have written a wonderful book that explores this extraordinary world beneath the waves off one of the most mysterious, and beautiful, of all African nations. It is a labour of love that displays not only genuine knowledge, but also a real affection for the country, its remarkable coastline, and of course its top-class diving. I commend it to you heartily.

Good luck!

Monty Halls
Managing Director, Seadog Productions

As the son of a United Nations ambassador, I travelled widely as a child and lived in many different countries. But it was Mozambique that stole my heart and I have chosen to live here since 1992.

I was stunned to discover the natural beauty of the Mozambican reefs and dived everywhere I could. In this way, I got to know the coast really well and through my many years in tourism have developed a very keen sense of what travellers are looking for and how to cater for their needs.

In my opinion Robynn and Ross's book hits the mark and provides precisely the kind of detail required when planning a diving trip to Mozambique. The coastline is so long that the diving varies considerably from one place to another, making it essential to have a comprehensive guide to enable divers to research where to find the type of diving they most enjoy.

From the sharks of Ponta do Ouro, to the whale sharks and mantas of Inhambane, to the fascinating creatures of Nampula to the exquisite beauty of the private islands of Cabo Delgado, the Bazaruto Archepelago and the Quirimbas, Mozambique offers it all. This book helps you find the diving that's right for you.

Martijn Mellaart
Director and Owner, Mozambique Voyages
www.mozambiquevoyages.com

MOZAMBIQUE
VOYAGES

Authors' preface

The seed for writing this book was planted many years ago when we watched a TV documentary by Monty Halls on diving in Mozambique. We were spellbound, having had no idea of the splendour just north of our home country, South Africa. We immediately decided to plan a dive trip to Mozambique and set out to find the definitive book on the subject to help us plan our visit. On discovering that there was no such book, we decided to write one.

Until now divers have had to depend on hit-and-miss Internet searches to gather information about diving in Mozambique. This information consisted largely of websites created by dive resorts, and it has been difficult to find objective or comparative information.

This book aims to resolve all that. It contains comprehensive information about all of the reliable dive resorts and dive centres in Mozambique. For each resort, we have tried to answer the questions that divers typically ask when choosing where to go on their next diving adventure:

❑ How large are the dive groups?
❑ How far are the dives from the launch site?
❑ What boats does the resort use?
❑ What is the sea temperature?
❑ Which are the best months for seeing a particular marine animal?
❑ When is the rainy season in a given area?
❑ What is the maximum permitted dive time?

The book also highlights how varied the diving is along Mozambique's extensive coastline. What is it that you are looking for? Whether it's mantas and whale sharks, shore diving with fabulous photographic opportunities, or adrenaline diving with sharks and strong currents, you will find it in Mozambique, and this book will assist you in choosing where and when to go.

Robynn and Ross Hofmeyr
Cape Town 2017

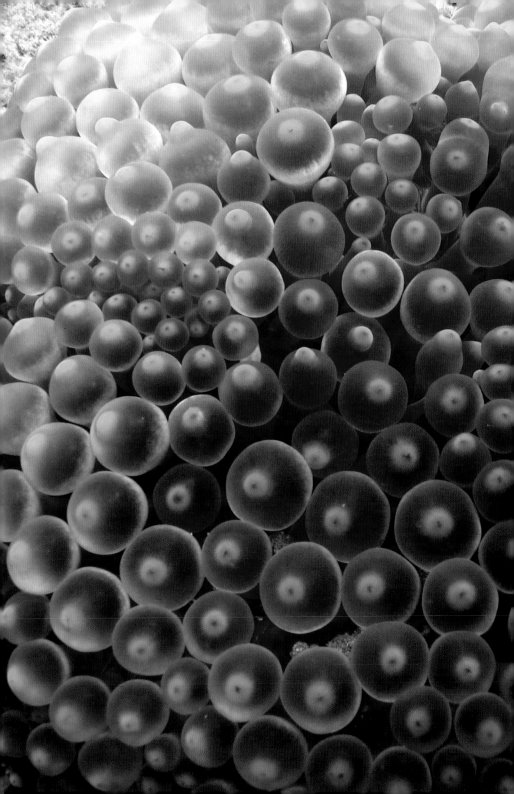

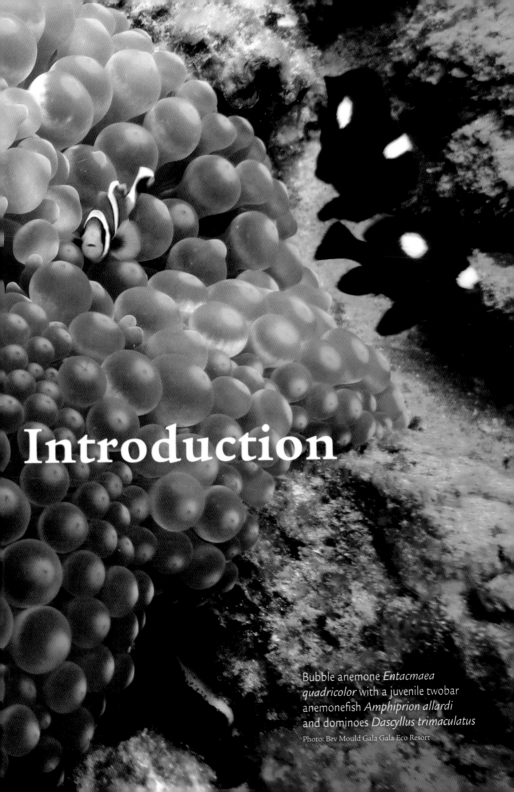

Introduction

Bubble anemone *Entacmaea
quadricolor* with a juvenile twobar
anemonefish *Amphiprion allardi*
and dominoes *Dascyllus trimaculatus*
Photo: Bev Mould Gala Gala Eco Resort

The breathtaking beauty of Mozambique's undersea world has until recently not been widely known about; but the diving community is rapidly discovering its attractions. For a long time the country's 2,000km coastline was inaccessible owing to civil war. When this finally ended in 1992, it left the country shattered, with very little infrastructure on which to build a sustainable future. In the years that followed, the outside world slowly started to explore the country, and Mozambique is now emerging as one of the top diving destinations in the world. The pristine, unspoilt reefs vary from stunningly beautiful to rugged and otherworldly. The colour and variety of the corals are astonishing, and the abundance and diversity of the marine life is unsurpassed anywhere in the world.

Mozambique has 11 provinces, of which seven are coastal. Only four of these currently have dive resorts. From north to south they are Cabo Delgado, Nampula, Inhambane and Maputo Province. This book is arranged accordingly – in four sections, north to south, with the dive resorts in each province also arranged roughly from north to south. The two archepelagos, Quirimbas and Bazaruto, are included with the provinces adjacent to which they lie.

Bordered roboastra *Roboastra luteolineata* and golden blenny *Ecsenius midas*

TRAVELLING TO MOZAMBIQUE

In March 2017, the government of Mozambique announced that visitors to the country are now eligible for 30-day tourist visas at those border posts equipped to issue biometric visas, namely:

- ❑ Maputo Airport
- ❑ Inhambane Airport
- ❑ Vilanculos Airport
- ❑ Beira Airport
- ❑ Tete Airport
- ❑ Nampula Airport
- ❑ Nacala Airport
- ❑ Pemba Airport
- ❑ Ponta do Ouro Border (South Africa)
- ❑ Goba Border (Swaziland)
- ❑ Nama Acha Border (Swaziland)
- ❑ Ressano Garcia Border (South Africa)
- ❑ Giriyondo Border (South Africa)

The announcement also stated that high commissions and consulates would no longer be issuing 30-day tourist visas, reinforcing the point that border visas are open to all visitors whether or not there is Mozambican representation in their home country.

HEALTH AND SAFETY

Most people travelling to exotic destinations on diving adventures worry about rare problems like decompression sickness, dread diseases and envenomation by marine creatures like jellyfish or stonefish. In fact, you are far more likely to suffer from traveller's diarrhoea, sunburn or an ear infection, which will ruin your diving holiday just as badly as having to spend time in a recompression chamber. For all of these conditions, prevention is better than cure.

The following are some general health precautions. For more detailed information, see the appendix on p.152.

- ❑ The public health service is often rudimentary and there are no recompression chamber facilities in reliable operation in Mozambique, so make sure that you have purchased health and evacuation insurance and that you are covered for 'adventure activities' such as scuba diving.
- ❑ Good hygiene, including strict hand washing, being cautious in using local water sources and taking probiotics or eating yoghurt with live cultures will reduce the risk of gastrointestinal upsets.

FLYING TO AND WITHIN MOZAMBIQUE

We have found South African Airlink to be by far the most reliable way of getting to and from Mozambique. Airlink (**www.flyairlink.com**) is a regional feeder airline operating as a franchisee to South African Airways (SAA). Thus Airlink travellers can connect conveniently with SAA, partner airlines and other carriers throughout southern Africa and the world. Airlink offers a network of regional and domestic flights within southern Africa, to 35 destinations in nine African countries, and is a member of the SAA loyalty programme (Voyager). Direct scheduled flights operate between Johannesburg and Beira, Maputo, Nampula, Pemba, Tete and Vilanculos.

A useful travel tip: When flying to Mozambican towns you will usually transfer to a very small plane. When you do so, the airline will ask you to hand in your hand luggage, as it is usually too big to fit into the tiny overhead compartments. If you have valuables in this bag, ask for a plastic bag that you can take on board with you and either fit into the overhead compartment or put at your feet, which is allowed. Do not check in your valuables.

For transport anywhere between Maputo and Inhassoro, contact Tofo Transfer Service (Marc Easton +258 849 111 884 or **marc73Easton@gmail.com**).

- Make sure to cover up, wear sunscreen and take sunglasses with UV protection.
- Swimmer's ear is common in areas with high humidity, so be careful to rinse and dry the ears after each dive. Alcohol-containing eardrops are useful too.
- Take particular care during beach launches and landings and when walking or wading across exposed reefs. It is sensible to have a small first-aid kit with plasters, antiseptic ointment, painkillers, and so forth.
- Remember to pack any regular medications you require, including treatments for motion sickness, if you suffer from it.
- Take measures to prevent being bitten by mosquitoes, such as covering exposed skin with long sleeves and trousers, moving indoors at dawn and dusk, using insect repellant, mosquito screens and nets. You can also take a plug-in electrical mosquito repellant with you.
- Malaria prophylaxis is very important. A good choice is doxycycline (Doximal®/Vibramycin®/Cyclidox®), which is considered safe for divers. It is one of the most reliable drugs and the most commonly recommended in areas with chloroquine-resistant malaria, such as Mozambique.

> **Note that some malaria prophylactics are unsuitable for divers (see p.156).**

- Make sure that your routine vaccinations are up to date. Although the risk of infection by Zika virus is low, pregnant women should consider the risk of travel to the area very carefully.
- Do not threaten or provoke dangerous animals. Observe from a safe distance. The treatment for stings depends on the offending species – see p.158.
- Don't dive if you have a cold or flu.
- Many dives feature strong currents, so good buoyancy control and being fit enough to kick hard for short distances are important.

Niarro Lodge

A slow ascent after a dive

ABBREVIATIONS USED IN THIS BOOK

Some important terms and abbreviations used in the book:

AI: Assistant Instructor

CMAS: Confédération Mondiale des Activités Subaquatiques, the international umbrella organisation for underwater sports, both competitive and recreational

Deco: Decompression time

Divers' house: A big house where divers stay cheaply, usually sharing rooms, a kitchen and a living area

DM: Divemaster

DSD: Discover Scuba Diving

HSA: Health and Safety Authorities

IANTD: International Association of Nitrox and Technical Divers

IDC: Instructor Development Course

Macro life: Very small sea critters

MSDT: Master Scuba Dive Trainer

PADI: Professional Association of Diving Instructors

RIB: Rigid inflatable boat

SDI: Scuba Diving International

SSI: Scuba Schools International

Swim-through: A place where divers can swim through a hole or crack between rocks

TDI: Technical Diving International

Vis: Visibility

Medjumbe Island, showing the
surrounding wealth of coral reefs
Photo: Minor Hotels

Cabo Delgado Province & The Quirimbas Archipelago

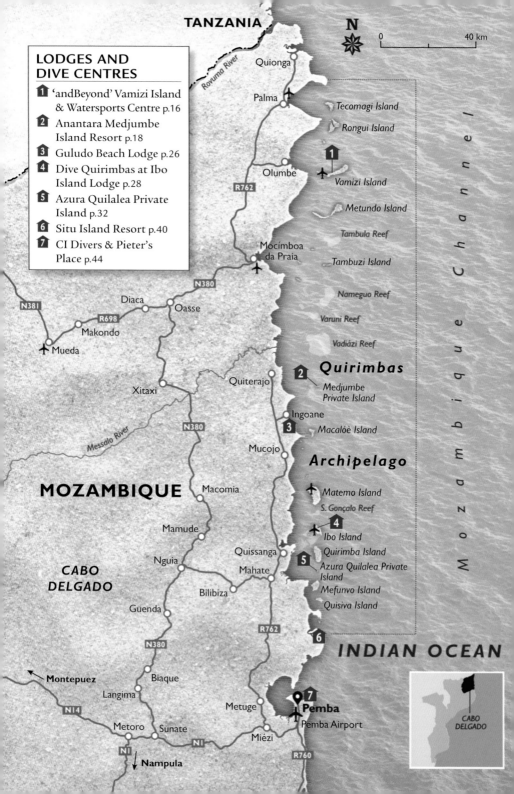

TANZANIA

N

0   40 km

Rovuma River

Quionga

Palma

LODGES AND DIVE CENTRES

1 'andBeyond' Vamizi Island & Watersports Centre p.16
2 Anantara Medjumbe Island Resort p.18
3 Guludo Beach Lodge p.26
4 Dive Quirimbas at Ibo Island Lodge p.28
5 Azura Quilalea Private Island p.32
6 Situ Island Resort p.40
7 CI Divers & Pieter's Place p.44

Tecomagi Island

Rongui Island

Olumbe

1

Vamizi Island

R762

Metundo Island

Tambula Reef

Tambuzi Island

Mocímboa da Praia

Nameguo Reef

Varuni Reef

Vadiázi Reef

N380

Diaca

Oasse

N381

R698

Makondo

Mueda

Xitaxi

Messalo River

N380

Quiterajo

2 *Quirimbas*

Medjumbe Private Island

Ingoane

3

Macaloè Island

Mucojo

Archipelago

MOZAMBIQUE

Macomia

Matemo Island

S. Gonçalo Reef

Mamude

4

Ibo Island

Nguia

Quissanga

Mahate

Quirimba Island

5

Azura Quilalea Private Island

CABO DELGADO

Bilibiza

Mefunvo Island

Quisiva Island

Guenda

R762

6

INDIAN OCEAN

N380

Biaque

Montepuez

Langima

Metuge

7

Pemba

Metoro

Sunate

Miézi

Pemba Airport

N14

N1

N1

R760

Nampula

CABO DELGADO

Mozambique Channel

Newly hatched turtles off Azura Quilalea

Cabo Delgado is the most northerly province of Mozambique. To the east of it lies the Quirimbas Archipelago, comprising 32 islands that stretch southwards for approximately 200km. The islands, which are rich in marine life, run along the coast, some tenuously linked to the mainland by sand bars, coral reefs and mangroves.

The archipelago is considered outstanding for the diversity of its marine life and serves as an important nursery area for dolphins and whales.

The diving around the islands varies tremendously, with peaceful and beautiful coral gardens for beginners and photographers, and vast drop-offs with strong currents for experienced and adventurous divers.

The resorts on these private islands offer luxurious accommodation and state-of-the-art diving facilities. Often you and your companions will be the only people on the boat, and the only boat at a pristine dive site. In addition to the resorts on the islands, there are dive resorts on the mainland of Cabo Delgado, which tend to be more affordable.

As this region lies close to the equator, the weather is always warm, and the sea temperature varies between 24 and 28°C.

Depending on the season, the rich marine life includes humpback whales, Napoleon wrasse, dolphins, dugongs, game fish, turtles and many vividly colourful fish and corals.

The table that follows provides some broad guidelines on when to visit Cabo Delgado and the Quirimbas area and indicates what you are likely to see. For more specific information, check the tables for the individual dive resorts in their own sections.

WHEN TO VISIT	Sea temp	Wind/rain	Good vis	Whales	Dolphins	Nudibranchs
Jan	28°C	✔			✔	✔
Feb	28°C	✔			✔	✔
Mar	28°C	✔			✔	✔
Apr	28°C	✔			✔	✔
May	27°C		✔		✔	✔
Jun	26°C		✔	✔	✔	✔
Jul	25°C		✔	✔	✔	✔
Aug	24°C		✔	✔	✔	✔
Sep	24°C		✔	✔	✔	✔
Oct	25°C		✔		✔	✔
Nov	26°C				✔	✔
Dec	28°C	✔			✔	✔

Note: Whale sharks and mantas are very rarely sighted in this area.

'andBeyond'
Vamizi Island &
Watersports Centre

DIVE CENTRE AND RESORT

🐾 The 'andBeyond' resort and the Vamizi Watersports Centre are under separate management but serve each other's guests

🐾 The watersports centre is privately run, with well-maintained equipment

🐾 Well-qualified and friendly staff

🐾 Can cater for up to 25 divers

DIVES

Single or double tank: Single dives to nearby sites; distant sites are double dives with a light lunch in between.

Divers per group: 1–10

DMs per group: One DM and one Instructor

Centre to launch: Directly from the centre, but from the other side of the island (2km away) from late December to February

Boat ride to dive sites: 5–45 mins

End of dive policy: They try to allow every diver to stay down until 50 bar while still under the supervision of a DM.

Main attractions: Deep-water canyons, wall dives, a wide diversity of fish and corals, great vis, quite a few sharks, pelagics, large groupers and the rare green humphead parrotfish. Activities offered by the watersports centre include stand-up paddleboarding, sport and fly-fishing, snorkelling, Hobie Cat sailing, guided nature walks, local community visits, private in-room yoga and spa

Fish life is plentiful and colourful in this region.

Natural, unspoilt beauty and blue water

sessions, castaway picnics, seasonal excursions to see turtles nesting and hatching, kayaking, dhow sailing, ethical spearfishing, whale- and dolphin-watching, cruises, deep-sea fishing (trolling, jigging and popping). Fly-fishers must supply their own gear – the rest are catered for.

BOATS

🐾 3 x rigid-hulled inflatables
🐾 Oxygen on all dive trips

Diving off a dhow

ACCOMMODATION
The quiet and peaceful private villas are ideal for large families and groups – this is elegant and luxurious, barefoot chic!

GENERAL
Comprises: Independent watersports centre on a resort island
Website: www.vamizi.com and www.andbeyond.com
Email: vamizidivecentre@gmail.com
Nearest airport: Pemba International, then a one-hour charter flight, followed by a 30-min scenic drive to the villas
Operating since: 2005
Courses offered: PADI

Fresh air comfort

WHEN TO GO
The diving is good year-round. Pelagics are present August to December, whales from July to November and vis is best August to February. It is windy from late December to mid-February.

WHAT THEY SAY
We offer unique pristine reefs, deep-water canyons and incredible fish and coral diversity. We are exclusive, completely off the beaten track, in a remote location and offer the personal touch. This is five-star service with 10-star dives!

WHAT WE SAY
We have not yet dived with Vamizi.

Anantara Medjumbe Island Resort

DIVE CENTRE

🐾 Staff help you prepare for the dive and rinse all gear afterwards

🐾 Towels and water supplied on boats

🐾 Close to lodge and chalets

🐾 Top-quality, well-maintained equipment

DIVES

Single or double tank: As requested

Divers per group: Usually two, maximum six

DMs per group: One instructor

Centre to launch: At high tide, directly from dive centre; at low tide, 600m away; divers can walk or go by buggy

Boat ride to dive sites: 10–15 mins

Dive policy: Small groups, which usually stay together

End of dive policy: Each buddy team surfaces when the first diver gets to 50 bar.

Main attractions: Medjumbe has many dive sites of varying depths, and reef structures that will suit all qualification and experience levels. There are dive sites all around the island, some still undiscovered. Wall drops to 800m.

BOATS

🐾 1 x Gulf Craft 31

🐾 Oxygen on all boats

Shoal of crescent-tail bigeyes *Priacanthus hamrur*

Snorkelling off Medjumbe

An aerial view of Medjumbe

Sea view from the lodge

Beach pool villa

ACCOMMODATION

A quiet, peaceful, luxury resort on a small island. The 12 'beach pool villas' – beachfront cottages with their own pools – are just 10m from the sea. You can sit in the bath and watch the waves come in. Activities include kayaking, sailing, snorkelling, kneeboarding, kitesurfing, spa treatments, picnics, sunset cruising, dhow lessons and cruises, fishing, and sleep-outs on a sand bank under the stars in a gorgeous four-poster bed with a mosquito net.

GENERAL

Comprises: Luxury resort with dive centre and spa
Website: medjumbe.anantara.com; Anantara Medjumbe Island resort is part of Minor Hotels www.minorhotels.com
Email: medjumbe@anantara.com
Nearest airport: Pemba
Operating since: 2006
Courses offered: There is a permanent PADI instructor on the island, who gives courses from Discover Scuba Diving (DSD) to DM.

WHEN TO GO	Sea temp	Wind/rain	Good vis.	Whales	Dolphins	Turtles	Nudibranchs
Jan	28°C	✔	✔		✔	✔	✔
Feb	30°C	✔	✔		✔	✔	✔
Mar	30°C	✔	✔		✔	✔	✔
Apr	28°C		✔		✔	✔	✔
May	28°C		✔			✔	✔
Jun	26°C		✔			✔	✔
Jul	26°C		✔	✔		✔	✔
Aug	24°C		✔	✔		✔	✔
Sep	24°C	✔	✔	✔	✔	✔	✔
Oct	26°C		✔		✔	✔	✔
Nov	28°C		✔		✔	✔	✔
Dec	29°C	✔	✔		✔	✔	✔

Note: Turtles come to the island to lay their eggs on the beach, typically around mid-July. If you are really lucky this could happen on your own beach between your chalet and the sea. Sharks and whale sharks are unlikely to be encountered.

WHAT THEY SAY

We have stunning corals, untouched reefs, diverse fish species and an incredible wall dive for more experienced divers. Our average water temperature is 28°C. We usually see whales from July to September and visibility is best from April to December.

WHAT WE SAY

Unspoilt, natural, light, comfortable, luxurious, breathtakingly beautiful, quiet …

Everything on this tiny island has been carefully designed to make the most of the natural beauty.

It felt as if I had gone away to my own beach cottage. Every luxury was there, from the coffee machine to the comfortable pillows, to multiple options for keeping cool and fresh – air conditioning, a ceiling fan and a sliding net-door for allowing fresh air, but not mosquitoes, into my room. There are few mosquitoes on the island anyway, so it was a pleasure to be able to sleep without needing a net; I didn't see (or hear) a single mosquito during my stay.

There is strong reliable Wi-Fi throughout the resort, including in the chalets, where there is a desk/table with international plugs and the right height of chair, so that you can keep your computer permanently set up for your stay.

Always a great treat to be able to go from a cold dive straight to a hot bath. Lovely oval bath under a window overlooking the sea, which is a mere 10m away.

Taking a gentle walk around the island is a special pleasure here. Timing is everything: you can only get right around at low tide, and you might prefer to walk early or late to avoid the heat. The day's high and low tide times are posted on a board in the dining room. The walk is a beautiful easy stroll and takes about an hour with lots of photo stops. You won't need shoes. The shells are lovely.

Falling asleep listening to the gentle lap of the ocean – heaven.

DIVE SITE INFORMATION

NORTHERN DIVE SITES

Sambi Sambi
Sloping wall
Depth: 12–80m
Diver level: Advanced only
Highlights/Nature of dive: A dramatically sloping wall to approximately 100m, this reef is covered in both hard corals and beautiful maze corals. Napoleon wrasse are commonly seen on this dive as well as the occasional leopard shark, green and hawksbill turtles and Chinese grouper.

Rocha's Rocks
Sloping reef,
Depth: 12–30m
Diver level: Intermediate/advanced; deep/current
Highlights/Nature of dive: On the southern end of Sambi Sambi the reef becomes uneven, creating gullies and large coral mounds. This reef is colourful and rich in species. Unicornfish are often seen hanging in the current. An excellent dive for an incoming tide, when the game fish come out to feed on the smaller fusiliers.

Sambi Plateau
Coral garden
Depth: 3–16m
Diver level: All levels
Highlights/Nature of dive: A pretty reef on top of a coral mount rising from the deep. The focus is on macro life (i.e. requiring macro lenses for photography), with all the usual reef suspects. you can visit a cleaning station, where smaller fish clean bigger ones, or look for an exotic nudibranch or camouflaged stone-, paper- or scorpionfish.

Brereton's Contours
Shallow ridged reef
Depth: 8–14m
Diver level: All levels
Highlights/Nature of dive: A spectacular dive for novices and the seasoned diver alike. Divers can swim through clouds of beautiful goldies and over

Two whitespotted rockcod *Epinephelux coeruleopunctatus*

a kaleidoscope of hard and soft corals, enjoying the warm clear waters of the Quirimbas.

The Cliffs of Insanity
Vertical wall
Depth: 24–800m+
Diver level: Advanced only; deep/current
Highlights/Nature of dive: The diver is presented with overhangs and ledges rich in sea life. Caverns and crevices are encrusted with dazzlingly colourful hard and soft corals. Large morays, lionfish and dogtooth tuna can be seen here, as well as the occasional circling school of barracuda.

Bia Reef
Sloping reef
Depth: 10–24m
Diver level: All levels
Highlights/Nature of dive: The reef, measuring about 350m in length and 130m in width, houses an incredible variety of hard and soft corals, growing in large colonies along its margins and in central mounds of various sizes. In addition to the abundant and diverse coral reef fishes, divers can expect large numbers of schooling fusiliers. Predatory fishes, such as barracudas, trevallies and jacks, are attracted and may put on impressive hunting displays.

Nudibranch *Chromodoris hamiltoni*

The Edge of Reason
Vertical wall
Depth: 15–800m+
Diver level: Advanced only; deep/current
Highlights/Nature of dive: Along the edge of the Medjumbe Passage divers can experience the feeling of flight as the wall gives way to the deep blue waters beyond. The ledge runs from east to west and massive brindle bass are often seen here, as well as the occasional shark, including Zambezi, grey reef, blacktip reef and tiger sharks. You may even be lucky enough to see the elusive sailfish.

EXTRACTS FROM ROBYNN'S DIVE LOG

Dive #: 783 **Date:** 15th June 2016   **Dive Site:** Coral Garden
Temp: 26°C **Time:** 58 mins   **Depth:** 19m   **Rated:** 4

Just the very professional instructor and me. Hard to do this dive justice. Blue, blue water, with crystal clear vis.

Some of the most beautiful corals I have ever seen; such a variety of fish that I had the impression someone had shaken out Dennis King's book, *The Reef Guide*, into the ocean. Sheer beauty and colour everywhere you looked. I remember the exquisite markings of the checkerboard wrasse and a tiny (1cm) blue-yellow damsel in particular.

This is a relatively shallow dive, mostly around 14m, perfect for beginners and photographers and yet still enchanting for experienced divers. We had the added bonus of experiencing about 400 juvenile tuna circling us, then heading off, only to repeat the process later. Fabulous dive.

Dive #: 784 **Date:** 16th June 2016 **Dive Site:** Edge of Reason (Medjumbe Wall)
Temp: 26°C **Time:** 48 mins   **Depth:** 44m   **Rated:** 4

Great dive. The wall falls away to 800m, so looking down you see the inkiest of blue, with moving shapes that entice you to go and investigate. I saw two big groupers at 44m and spent a short while with them. The gorgonians are dramatic and lovely. Even after days of wind the vis was still quite good, and the current manageable. Stingrays, two very big scorpionfish and a turtle in the shallows.

Dive #: 785 **Date:** 16th June 2016   **Dive Site:** Laura's Leap
Temp: 27°C **Time:** 58 mins   **Depth:** 21m   **Rated:** 3

We chose this dive because it is known as a fast-drift dive. Murphy's Law — there was virtually no current. In the first minute of the dive we saw a turtle. There are not many corals there, and I thought the dive might be a dud, but then we started finding things. Two juvenile emperor angelfish — my favourite fish! One was so tiny (about 3cm) that it's hard to believe so much beauty could be packed into so small a space. Morays of every description: green, honeycomb, brown, geometric. Two anemone crabs; three lionfish; tiny angelfish.

Laura's Leap

Vertical wall

Depth: 12–1,200m+

Diver level: Advanced only; deep/current

Highlights/Nature of dive: In the middle of the Medjumbe Passage lies Laura's Leap, a narrow channel where the current will take you flying along the edge of the abyss. The wall is pocketed with large caves and overhangs and peppered with massive gorgonian sea fans. Groupers rest together in large schools in the caves.

Dennis King

Regal angelfish *Pygoplites diacanthus*

Dive #: 786	Date: 17th June 2016		Dive Site: Cliffs of Insanity
Temp: 26°C	Time: 48 mins	Depth: 40m	Rated: 4

Dropped into the deep, deep blue to 40m. Felt like flying. Lots to see on the wall. Slowly made our way back up so that no extra deco. time was incurred. On the way up I allowed the current to carry me back over the edge of the wall so that I was surrounded by nothing but the deep blue. Wonderful sensation.

Dive #: 787	Date: 18th June 2016		Dive Site: Coral Gallery *
Temp: 26°C	Time: 92 mins	Depth: 6.3m	Rated: 5

What a dive. It's not often I rate a dive a 5, so this was something exceptional. Dropped into crystal-clear water and a world of multicoloured corals. There were brightly coloured fish of every description everywhere I looked. I had the sense of having gone to another place, one of extreme beauty and colour. Every fish looked like a living work of art, moving among stunning corals.

At one stage we were in a sort of coral amphitheatre. When we looked up there was a swirl of moving colour. At least 1,000 fish were swimming in a circle around us, many dark blue velvet surgeons set against bright yellow convict surgeons, light blue powder surgeons and the stunning lines of Moorish idols. We hung in the water, entranced.

At 60 minutes I asked the dive guide if we should go up. He responded by asking me if I was cold or hungry and when I said no he offered to carry on with the dive. Doesn't happen often! We continued on and saw a turtle, four boxfish, many butterflyfish, my first two horsefish *Congiopodus torvus* and way too many others to name.

Later on, the swirling circle formed again, but this time with about double the number of fish. One of those unique moments you know you will never forget. We finally called it quits at 92 minutes for the sake of the skipper. The Quirimbas has fabulous diving, but this one stands out as one of the best.

* The Coral Gallery reef was only recently discovered. I was lucky to be among the first people to dive it.

A rare sighting of a manta *Manta alfredi*; this species uses its front 'arms' to scoop up plankton.

SOUTHERN DIVE SITES
Joe's Ridge
Fringing reef
Depth: 9–14m
Diver level: All levels
Highlights/Nature of dive: At Joe's Ridge the coral reef forms ridges interspersed with sandy patches. In the azure waters here you will find resident fish such as sweetlips, puffers, angelfish and triggerfish. Turtles also rest here on their way out to deeper waters.

Shallow Hal's
Fringing reef
Depth: 8–12m
Diver level: All levels
Highlights/Nature of dive: The shallow waters clearly show the true colours of the coral and reef fish that inhabit this area. Juvenile fish seeking sanctuary from the open sea frequent ornate structures and formations in the coral rocks. Anemones filter the water and the resident 'Nemos' (clownfish) never stray far from home.

Dusky Pinnacle
Coral bank
Depth: 8–15m
Diver level: All levels
Highlights/Nature of dive: This small coral mound with gradually sloping edges is easily circumnavigated in a single dive. The hard coral forms archways and chimneys, which gives this site its name. On the sandy seabed you may come across fan-tailed stingrays, camouflaged crocodilefish, scorpionfish and lionfish.

Sita's Hollow
Coral bank
Depth: 10–18m
Diver level: Intermediate; rough surface conditions
Highlights/Nature of dive: Three small coral banks lie in close proximity to each other. This site is comprised predominantly of hard corals rising from a sandy base. Schooling fish species gather across the reef.

Neptune's Nursery
Coral bank
Depth: 8–15m
Diver level: All levels
Highlights/Nature of dive: This hard coral reef offers shelter for a wide variety of fish species and is a hunting ground for game fish. The site is relatively level, with intricate hard-coral structures to explore. Schools of fusiliers, small snappers and juvenile sweetlips, bluespotted stingrays, unusual ribbon eels and flamboyant nudibranchs of every shape and colour can be found here.

Quarmby Reef
Coral garden
Depth: 16m
Diver level: Advanced only; current; challenging surface conditions
Highlights/Nature of dive: An extensive coral plateau. Soft corals in a wide array of colours and textures. Vibrant angelfish, butterflyfish and altheas, large kingfish, barracuda and jobfish pass by in search of food or a quick stop at a cleaning station. Nudibranchs and mantis shrimps are commonly found here as well.

A LETTER FROM MEDJUMBE

Female loggerhead turtle heading for the sea

Her tracks

Dear Robynn

Exciting news today! Usually green turtles lay at Medjumbe but today it was a different visitor! Around eight this morning, we were alerted that a mother loggerhead turtle was laying eggs on the beach not far from the lighthouse. The guests left their breakfast to come and see this special sight.

The mother turtle was exhausted and on her way back to the ocean, which was far, as the tide was still coming in. She had about 100m left to walk. We could see she was tired. She stopped regularly, and was becoming dehydrated. The staff gently poured water over her to keep her cool.

All the guests were cheering, encouraging her on. It took her about an hour to make it all the way to the ocean, struggling down the sand and stopping regularly to catch her breath.

Finally the ocean met her halfway. The final metres were difficult, and she rested her head in the water to recover. After a while, reunited with her beloved ocean, she swished her limbs and went flying through the water again, until next time.

Kind regards

Anne

Close-up of the exhausted female

At last she makes it to the water.

Guludo Beach Lodge

DIVE CENTRE

🐾 On the beach

DIVES

Single or double tank: Usually two dives per trip
Divers per group: Usually 2–4, maximum of six
DMs per group: One DM
Centre to launch: About 6 mins
Boat ride to dive sites: 15–20 mins
Dive policy: Small groups, so all stay together
End of dive policy: DM usually goes up with the first diver to reach 50 bar
Main attractions: Beautiful coral, many game fish, turtles and reef sharks. There are sites suitable for all levels: great, easy diving around Rolas Island for beginners and photographers, and advanced diving at Zala Atoll.

BOATS

🐾 2 x RIBs
🐾 Oxygen on all boats

A green turtle *Chelonia midas* at Zala Atoll

Ternate chromis *Chromis ternatensis* with shoal of bluebanded snappers *Lutjanus kasmira*

Activities include dhow safaris.

WHEN TO GO	Sea temp	Wind/rain	Good vis	Whales	Dolphins	Sharks	Nudibranchs
Jan	26°C	✔	✔		✔	✔	✔
Feb	27°C	✔	✔		✔	✔	✔
Mar	27°C	✔	✔		✔	✔	✔
Apr	26°C	✔	✔		✔	✔	✔
May	25°C		✔		✔	✔	✔
Jun	24°C		✔		✔	✔	✔
Jul	24°C			✔	✔	✔	✔
Aug	24°C			✔	✔	✔	✔
Sep	25°C		✔	✔	✔	✔	✔
Oct	25°C		✔	✔	✔	✔	✔
Nov	26°C		✔	✔	✔	✔	✔
Dec	26°C			✔		✔	✔

Note: Whale sharks and mantas are seldom encountered.

ACCOMMODATION

The resort is quiet, peaceful and suitable for families. Eco-aware, barefoot luxury in beachfront bandas. Activities include island trips, dhow safaris, bush walks, beach archery, village trips and bush lookouts.

GENERAL

Comprises: Resort with own dive centre
Website: www.guludo.com
Email: enquiries@guludo.com
Nearest airport: Pemba
Operating since: 2006
Courses offered: PADI

WHAT THEY SAY

We have 12km of white sandy beach to ourselves. Some income from each guest goes to the local community and benefits conservation projects such as school feeding schemes and reef and whale surveys.

WHAT WE SAY

Please note that we have not yet dived with Guludo.

Outside view of a beachfront banda

A humpback whale *Megaptera novaeangliae* breaching

Dive Quirimbas at Ibo Island Lodge

DIVE CENTRE

- Situated 100m from the beach
- Water provided on the boats
- Staff prepare the gear and load and offload the boat

DIVES

Single or double tank: Usually two dives per trip; single dives on request

Divers per group: Usually 2–4, maximum six

DMs per group: One instructor

Centre to launch: Gentle flat-water launch from pier, 4 mins' walk from centre

Boatride to dive sites: 20–30 mins on the speedboats, 1–1.5 hours on the dhows

End of dive policy: All divers come up together

Main attractions: Pristine coral reefs at 25m or less; macro life, seasonal whales, a huge diversity of reef fish and plenty of turtles

BOATS

- 3 x dhows
- 1 x RIB
- Oxygen on all boats

Flatworm *Thysanozoon* sp.

©www.smistyfish.co.za 2011

An aerial view of Ibo Island

Ibo Island Lodge

WHEN TO GO	Sea temp	Wind/rain	Good vis	Whales	Dolphins	Nudibranchs
Jan	29°C	✔	✔		✔	✔
Feb	29°C	✔	✔		✔	✔
Mar	28°C		✔		✔	✔
Apr	27°C		✔		✔	✔
May	26°C		✔		✔	✔
Jun	25°C	✔			✔	✔
Jul	24°C	✔		✔	✔	✔
Aug	24°C	✔		✔	✔	✔
Sep	25°C	✔		✔	✔	✔
Oct	26°C		✔	✔	✔	✔
Nov	27°C		✔		✔	✔
Dec	28°C	✔	✔		✔	✔

Note: Mantas, sharks and whale sharks are seldom encountered. Rains occur between December and February, and it is windiest from June to September.

A verandah at the lodge

The pool at Ibo Island Lodge

ACCOMMODATION
The lodge is a grand old historical building. It is quiet, peaceful and suitable for families. Activities include dolphin safaris, snorkelling, kayaking, bird-watching, historical tours, massages, sailing dhows, island hopping and mangrove trips. They also offer live-aboard charters for up to four divers on a 40-foot catamaran throughout the Quirimbas, including Lazarus Banks.

GENERAL
Comprises: Dive centre and accommodation
Website: www.divequirimbas.com
Email: reservations@iboisland.com

Nearest airport: Pemba; then to Ibo Island's airstrip via private plane or helicopter
Operating since: 2012
Courses offered: PADI

WHAT THEY SAY
We are the only dive centre on Ibo Island and you will not see other boats or divers. The diversity of the corals and marine life is amazing.

WHAT WE SAY
Ibo Island is different: one of the oldest inhabited islands in the Quirimbas Archipelago, its recorded history dates back to 600AD,

Guide Anli in front of the old slave fort

when Omani traders established contact with the locals. Centuries of battle for ownership of this strategically positioned island culminated in Portuguese rule in the 1700s. Sadly, slavery was big business, and evidence of this trade still haunts the island.

Ibo Island's residents live a simple life, surviving hand to mouth and doggedly eking out a hard existence by fishing. Many were born here and want no other life. It's a place where family means everything, and where the island life is valued more highly than the comforts of city living. Currently, about 6,000 people stay on Ibo, and they all seem to know one another.

After the Portuguese left in the early 1900s, the old stone town took on the look of a ghost town, full of abandoned and collapsing buildings.

In the 1700s the buildings now comprising Ibo Island Lodge were government offices and a private house. When Kevin and Fiona Record found them, in the late 1990s, they were 'roofless lime and coral stone ruins, swaying in the wind'. The couple fell in love with Ibo and

set out to build a lodge that would also bring some employment to the local people.

Today, the buildings have been beautifully restored and convey a sense of colonial grandeur, with huge rooms, high ceilings, wide, furnished verandahs, sweeping lawns, and rooms filled with exquisite furniture, some of which was painstakingly and expertly made on the island.

Staying in the lodge, it feels as if you have strayed into an Agatha Christie novel, and one half expects to meet Hercule Poirot at tea.

There are three swimming pools, monkeys in the garden and a rooftop restaurant overlooking the sea. There is also free (if temperamental) Wi-Fi.

Tourism has brought a new source of income to Ibo Island. Your visit there will make a difference. Be sure to do the history tour with guide Anli. You will pass silversmiths working quietly, creating exquisite and reasonably priced jewellery that makes a wonderful reminder of this unique island. However, do take some meticais with you, as they do not accept credit cards and the single ATM on the island is unreliable at best.

Bluebanded snappers *Lutjanus kasmira* swim over a cabbage coral on the Ibo Lighthouse dive.

EXTRACTS FROM ROBYNN'S DIVE LOG

Dive #: 781   **Date:** 11th June 2016   **Dive Site:** Lighthouse Reef
Temp: 26°C   **Time:** 65 mins   **Depth:** 19m   **Rated:** 4

Just me, an instructor and a DM. Dropped into the bluest blue. Although the wind had blown sand into the water over the past few days, once you were within 2m or so of the reef, it was as clear as crystal. A truly fabulous site. Colour everywhere, with many different fish and corals. The calm was jolted by the biggest cobia any of us had ever seen — we guessed it was about 2m. Also saw two gorgeous purple paperfish and two tiny pipefish.

Dive #: 782   **Date:** 14th June 2016   **Dive Site:** Matemo Reef
Temp: 26°C   **Time:** 62 mins   **Depth:** 20m   **Rated:** 3

Wind has been blowing for days, so sea unsettled and vis not marvellous. Again, however, within 2–3m of the reef we could see very clearly. Marc found an octopus hiding under some rocks. I saw two of the smallest trumpetfish I've ever seen, each about 7cm long. Pretty bommies with zillions of fish — scissors, blue chromis, goldies, yellowtail goldies, butterflies, vagabond butterflies, chocolate dips, Moorish idols, fusiliers, sweetlips, dominos, adorned wrasses, titan triggerfish and a juvenile Napoleon.

Common octopus

Azura Quilalea Private Island

DIVE CENTRE

- On the beach
- Tea, coffee and water provided
- Towels and water on all boats
- Close to lodge and villas
- No nitrox

DIVES

Single or double tank: Usually single, but will do doubles by arrangement

Divers per group: Maximum six

DMs per group: One dive leader

Centre to launch: Directly from dive centre

Boat ride to dive sites: About 5–15 mins

Dive policy: Dive as a group in buddy pairs, following guide who has a buoy line

End of dive policy: All divers come up when first diver reaches 50 bar

Main attractions: World-class hard and soft corals, walls, caverns, reef gardens, schooling jacks, kingfish, fusiliers, snappers, Napoleon wrasse, stingrays, lionfish, turtles, moray eels, occasional grey reef sharks, brindle bass and macro critters

BOATS

- 1 x W32 Libra Banana Boat
- 1 x Novacat 220 (Sirius) 6.9m
- DAN oxygen on boats

In addition to the house reef shown here, there are numerous other dive sites to visit.

An aerial view of Azura Quilalea

The African Spa offers relaxing treatments.

ACCOMMODATION
A quiet, peaceful, 'barefoot luxury' resort, located on a small private island, with everything right on the beach. Children are welcome. Activities include snorkelling, fishing, kayaking, birding and visits to the spa.

GENERAL
Comprises: Private island resort with spa, watersports and dive centre
Website: www.azura-retreats.com
Email: reservations@azura-retreats.com
Nearest airport: Pemba; the resort is 30 nautical miles north, by helicopter or private plane.
Operating since: 2012
Courses offered: PADI

One of the seafront villas

WHEN TO GO	Sea temp	Wind/rain	Good vis	Whales	Dolphins	Sharks	Nudibranchs
Jan	28°C	✔			✔		✔
Feb	28°C	✔			✔		✔
Mar	28°C	✔			✔		✔
Apr	28°C	✔			✔		✔
May	27°C		✔		✔		✔
Jun	26°C		✔		✔		✔
Jul	25°C		✔	✔	✔		✔
Aug	24°C		✔	✔	✔		✔
Sep	24°C		✔	✔	✔		✔
Oct	25°C		✔		✔		✔
Nov	26°C				✔		✔
Dec	28°C	✔			✔		✔

Note: Whale sharks are unlikely to be encountered, but turtles may be seen.

WHAT THEY SAY

Azura Quilalea lies within a marine reserve and offers world-class snorkelling and diving on the protected house reef and outer fringe reefs. The resort accommodates a maximum of 18 guests at a time, which guarantees exclusive diving, attention to detail and a sense of privacy. Azura Quilalea's unique selling point is the easily accessible house reef, right off the main beach, just a few steps away from the dive centre.

Coral bommie

WHAT WE SAY

You realise straightaway that things are going to be different on this beautiful island when you are greeted on the beach not only by management but also by your own private butler, who has made you a lei out of local palm fronds. The hospitality and luxury here are unsurpassed.

Each spacious villa has its own private beach, daybeds, a hammock, inside and outside showers, fans, air conditioning, a vast comfortable bed with Egyptian cotton bedding and soft pillows, a huge mosquito net over the bed and side tables, tea, filter coffee, stocked minibar, fridge with fresh milk, champagne and a jar of freshly baked shortbread biscuits.

There is no fresh water on the island, which means that there are very few mosquitoes. The island water is desalinated, very pure and drinkable directly from the taps if you wish, although there are attractive glass bottles of drinking water everywhere.

It's well worthwhile going for a kayak in the mangroves. If you're especially lucky, you may see monkeys. The silence is awe-inspiring.

A luxurious spa, situated in a big rock cave, overlooks the sea. The therapist has healing hands, and it is pure pleasure to have her ease

Enjoying a sunset bubble bath and cocktail, while watching the sun go down

The path around the island

away the tension while you listen to the gentle rhythm of the waves.

You may enjoy taking a walk right around the island. Ask for a map that you can carry with you, as there are many paths. You'll need casual shoes such as slip slops. The walk is just over an hour if you stroll, and you'll probably want to take your camera so that you can photograph the turtle beach, baobab trees, herons, whales (in season) and quiet forest paths.

It is very hard to leave this place.

Kayaking in the mangroves

Sunset at Quilalea beach bar

Colour in the deep blue

Male (blue) and female (yellow) ribbon eels
Rhinomuraena quaesita

DIVE SITE INFORMATION

Azura Quilalea House Reef

One of the few house reefs in Mozambique with an easy shore entry; this dive site is usually open only to guests of Azura Quilalea.

Entry: Shore entry from Azura Quilalea's main beach

Diver level: Discover Scuba Diver-friendly; open water

Average depth: 14m

Maximum depth: 18m

Highlights/Nature of dive: Predominantly hard corals, with a sandy bottom. A long narrow reef with ribbon eels, moray eels in their hideouts, cleaner shrimps, glassfish, nudibranchs and sea slugs, lionfish, batfish, Moorish idols, fusiliers, saladfish, octopus, small and large groupers, bluespotted stingrays and a great variety of schooling fish, often being hunted by bluefin kingfish. Green turtles are frequently seen resting on the reef, and you might see a friendly resident hawksbill turtle, unperturbed by divers. To the north, cleaner shrimps at a small cleaning station are often willing to give divers a delightful 'manicure'. This reef is an exceptionally productive dive site.

The Canyon

An action-packed current dive accessed by boat

Entry: Boat dive

Diver level: Open water for the shallow canyon; advanced for the deeper canyon

Average depth: 18–22m

Maximum depth: 30m

Highlights/Nature of dive: Characterised by overhangs with colourful corals, the deeper side of The Canyon features whip corals interspersed with colourful soft corals that camouflage nudibranchs and a host of other macro delights. Threespot angelfish, large honeycomb morays and both green and hawksbill turtles are commonly seen, while sightings of fire gobies and scissortail gobies are possible. The strong currents flowing through an area called the 'runway' attract many fish, and divers can find shelter in rock crevices at 14m, and look out for large brindle bass, bigeye kingfish, barracuda, snappers, unicornfish, giant trevally, Napoleon wrasse and grey reef shark. During the safety stop look out for the many fish frequenting the hard and soft corals covering the top of the reef. Vis is variable, depending on the current.

Casino

A deep, action-packed current dive

Entry: Boat dive

Diver level: Advanced

Average depth: 20–35m

Maximum depth: 35m

An eye-catching coral at Casino

Honeycomb moray *Gymnothorax favagineus*

Highlights/Nature of dive: Characterised by unusually large schools of batfish and many green turtles. Overhangs with large gorgonian fans, colourful corals, including whip corals and coral-encrusted bommies. Large fields of lettuce coral covered in juvenile yellow snappers. This site is best dived on the incoming tide. Visibility is usually good and there is much to be seen.

Ponta Wall

About 30 mins to reach, this is the furthest dive site from Azura Quilalea.

Entry: Boat dive

Diver level: Open water/advanced

Average depth: 11–25m

Maximum depth: 30m

Highlights/Nature of dive: Vis tends to be good year-round, and the 30m-deep seabed is often visible from the boat. The top of the wall starts at 12m, with a sheer drop down to 30m. The current can vary from none to very strong. The site is characterised by overhangs with caverns, covered with glassfish; also typical at this site are Napoleon wrasse, large schools of Russell's snapper and schools of rubberlips and batfish. Whitetip reef sharks are usually seen at the rocky bottom of the wall. A highlight towards the end of the dive, current permitting, is a leisurely swim-through, with an entrance at 25m, which emerges into a coral garden at the top of the reef, at 12m. There is also an 'amphitheatre' formation, which attracts large schools of yellow snapper and surgeonfish.

Claudia Pellarini/Azura Quilalea

Gorgonian fans, Family Plexauridae

Mefumvo Wall

The deepest wall dive in the area
Entry: Boat dive
Diver level: Advanced
Average depth: 15–20m
Maximum depth: 35m
Highlights/Nature of dive: The deepest of
all the wall dives in the area, reaching 35m in
some places. Characterised by overhangs with
caverns that extend into the reef for a few
metres, inside which are resident groupers
and stingrays as well as large schools of red
snapper. Occasionally whitetip reef sharks can
be seen resting in the sand in deeper water.

Quissiva Wall

Combination of a wall and coral gardens
Entry: Boat dive
Diver level: Open water/advanced
Average depth: 15–20m
Maximum depth: 22m
Highlights/Nature of dive: A vertical wall to
16m, then coral bommie formations with
reef gardens sloping down to 22m; occasional
sightings of Napoleon wrasse.

Sencar Wall – Sencar Shamba

Coral gardens running along a ridge of reef,
separated by large sandy patches
Entry: Boat dive
Diver level: Open water
Average depth: 10–15m
Maximum depth: 15m
Highlights/Nature of dive: On the open-ocean
side of Sencar Island, and best dived on the
high tide, this ridge is an expansive reef garden,
characterised by coral bommies and sand
patches, where turtles and Napoleon wrasse
are often sighted. Clown and redfang triggerfish
are common, as well as schools of surgeonfish,
which hover overhead; pelagics occasionally
pass by too. On the odd occasion, bottlenose
dolphins stop in to take a closer look at
the divers.

Sencar Wall – Mesundju Rocks

An expanse of rocky coral gardens along
a ridge of reef
Entry: Boat dive
Diver level: Open water
Average depth: 10–15m
Maximum depth: 25m
Highlights/Nature of dive: North of Sencar
Shamba lies this very similar ridge of reef, with
more rocky substrate than sandy bottom. The
fish life is much like that of Sencar Shamba
(see above).

Fusi Spot

Sloping reef gardens with optional wall
Entry: Boat dive
Diver level: Open water
Average depth: 10–20m
Maximum depth: 18–25m
Highlights/Nature of dive: A slightly sloping
reef; the coral gardens extend from a depth
of 7m to 18m at their westernmost point,
and there is a 25m wall on the eastern side
of the reef. Dolphins enjoy playing in this spot
and, if you're lucky, will approach you for a
closer look.

Salama Banks

A shallow reef dive
Entry: Boat dive
Diver level: Open water
Average depth: 10m
Maximum depth: 14m
Highlights/Nature of dive: The dive starts at 14m, where there is a wide range of coral bommies and reef fish. Green turtles are seen from time to time.

Freckled hawkfish *Paracirrhites forsteri*

Ridges

Three ridges in the open ocean
Entry: Boat dive
Diver level: Open water
Average depth: 10–15m
Maximum depth: 18m

Highlights/Nature of dive: Three open-ocean ridges run side by side within sight of each other here. There are large schools of snapper and a wide range of reef fish. You might also see pelagics passing by overhead.

EXTRACTS FROM ROBYNN'S DIVE LOG

| Dive #: 778 | Date: 9th June 2016 | | Dive Site: The Canyon |
| Temp: 26°C | Time: 48 mins | Depth: 26m | Rated: 4 |

Just the dive guide and me. Dropped down to about 24m. Poor vis but lots to see anyway. Very strong current. Big turtle, king mackerel, schools of fusiliers. Lovely corals. We allowed ourselves to be swept along quite fast – exhilarating. At one stage we held onto a ledge and watched the world go by, but the current was giving us mask issues, so we continued on our way. Nice dive; would like to do it again with good vis.

| Dive #: 779 | Date: 10th June 2016 | | Dive Site: Fusi Spot |
| Temp: 26°C | Time: 48 mins | Depth: 19m | Rated: 3 |

Very pretty dive. Lots of sediment in the water so vis iffy. Particularly beautiful corals. Bluespotted stingray under a rock, adult boxfish, bright butterflyfish everywhere.

| Dive #: 780 | Date: 10th June 2016 | | Dive Site: Azura Quilalea Housereef |
| Temp: 26°C | Time: 54 mins | Depth: 16m | Rated: 4 |

I really enjoyed this dive. So much to see, and we walked in from the beach, just a few metres from my breakfast table. Four ribbon eels, three bluespotted stingrays, three turtles, two nudibranchs, two flatworms, lots of yellowspotted kingfish and zillions of other brightly coloured fish. Bommies with goldies, chocolate dips and blue chromis everywhere. The dive guide showed me a station where cleaner shrimps sweetly nibbled at my fingers. Surprised to realise that in the same rock, about level with my face, was a huge moray, just watching me.

Situ Island Resort

DIVE CENTRE

- Staff prepare the gear, load and offload the boats and rinse out the divers' gear
- Divers check their own gear before the boat leaves

DIVES

Single or double tank: Usually two dives, with a surface interval on an island between dives
Divers per group: 2–8
Leaders per group: One leader. Please note that the dive leader is not a DM, but is highly experienced and has led many hundreds of dives at the island. Groups are welcome to bring their own DM if they prefer.
Centre to launch: Directly from centre
Boat ride to dive sites: 25 mins
Dive policy: Divers stay in a group, diving with a buddy. The dive leader has a surface marker buoy that is monitored from the boat.
End of dive policy: Small groups, relatively shallow dives (max 28m) and access to 15-litre tanks (if requested before arrival) mean that most dives are 60 mins.

Main attractions: All of the sites are in the Quirimbas National Park, so the reefs have been protected for many years. They have various wall dives and drop-offs with wonderful reef, tropical and game fish. You won't see other divers.

BOATS

- 1 x 38ft Supercat with 2 x 85 h.p. Yamaha motors
- 1 x 36ft Yamaha SeaSpirit with 2 x 100 h.p. 4-stroke Yamaha motors
- DAN oxygen kit on all dive trips

Situ's Supercat

Situ's colourful reefs have been protected for many years.

Relaxing on a sand spit between dives

ACCOMMODATION

A quiet, peaceful family resort. Simple, beachy, elegant. All eight chalets are directly on the beach. Also offers kayaking, nature trails, birding, leisure cruises, walks to the local village and boat trips to the surrounding islands and mangroves.

GENERAL

Comprises: Private island resort with its own dive centre
Website: www.situisland.com
Email: bookings@situisland.com
Nearest airport: Pemba, then 40km (about 70 mins) by sea to the island
Operating since: 2008
Courses offered: No

Sailing dhow

Beach chalet at sunset

View of the interior of a beach chalet

WHEN TO GO	Sea temp	Wind/rain	Good vis	Whales	Dolphins	Nudibranchs
Jan	30°C	✔			✔	✔
Feb	30°C	✔			✔	✔
Mar	29°C	✔			✔	✔
Apr	28°C		✔		✔	✔
May	27°C		✔		✔	✔
Jun	26°C		✔		✔	✔
Jul	26°C		✔		✔	✔
Aug	27°C				✔	✔
Sep	27°C		✔	✔	✔	✔
Oct	27°C			✔	✔	✔
Nov	28°C	✔	✔	✔	✔	✔
Dec	30°C	✔	✔		✔	✔

Note: Sharks, whale sharks and mantas are unlikely to be encountered.

Very Robinson Crusoe

Flatworm *Pseudoceros* sp.

WHAT THEY SAY

Situ is a private island resort with pristine reefs and unspoilt diving. Dive groups of six or more can bring their own DM, but we do offer the services of a dive guide. Good value for money. Groups of eight or more can have the entire island to themselves.

WHAT WE SAY

Situ is a small private island that might just have been discovered by Robinson Crusoe himself. Almost everything is built of wood and bamboo. There are only eight chalets, so there is never more than a small group of people at any time. In fact, Situ makes the offer that if you bring a group of eight or more they will close the island during your stay, giving your group total exclusivity.

Situ does not have a resident DM or Instructor, so groups often bring their own. However, Tess knows all the sites very well and is happy to guide dives if you don't bring your own DM. There is a small amount of good-quality dive gear, but bring your own if you have it, or check with Tess how many divers will be using their gear during your stay. There are two dive boats, both very comfortably equipped.

The chalets are spacious and well designed. Everything provided is of top quality. They have excellent mosquito nets, forming a virtual room around the king-sized bed and bedside tables, so that you have access to everything inside the net. There is no air conditioning, but the ample fans and open design of the chalets make it redundant.

Clown triggerfish *Balistoides conspicillum*

There is a large communal area, with different tables for breakfast, lunch and supper, and plenty of comfortable armchairs and couches.

Tess and Craig Macdonald are fabulous hosts, creating a friendly, relaxed atmosphere. Tess takes care of everyone and runs the diving. Craig cooks extremely tasty meals and is the skipper.

Broadbarred lionfish *Pteorois antennata*

The library, daily free washing service, always-available tea, coffee, rusks and drinks and decent Wi-Fi make Situ a home away from home.

Bluebanded snappers *Lutjanus kasmira*

EXTRACTS FROM ROBYNN'S DIVE LOG

Dive #: 776	Date: 5th June 2016		Dive Site: Dogtooth North, Situ Island
Temp: 27°C	Time: 55 mins	Depth: 20m	Rated: 4

Tess and I giant-strided off their Supercat into warm clear water. We sank to about 18m and into Fairyland. Interesting topography with huge rocks; the caves were covered with pristine corals of all shades. Big schools of fish everywhere. There was so much to see that you could stay in one place for ages. In addition to the usual Indian Ocean fish, we saw a juvenile rockmover wrasse (my first), which looks as if it has an extra fin pointing upwards, a clown triggerfish, a juvenile oriental sweetlips gyrating, and a striking Linda's flatworm.

Dive #: 777	Date: 6th June 2016		Dive Site: Buntings
Temp: 26°C	Time: 55 mins	Depth: 19.2m	Rated: 4

Just Tess and me again. First thing we saw on descending was a whitetip reef shark. Otherwise, the dive was similar to yesterday's, but with more of everything. Bigger schools, more schools, stunningly coloured corals and fish. Perhaps a nursery too, as we saw many juveniles. Tiny scythe triggerfish, battling to balance in the current, two tiny trumpetfish hiding in the corals, both juvenile and adult black beauties, clown triggers, zillions of snappers, brilliant yellow butterflyfish, a school of surgeonfish and some saddleback hogfish.

Situ dive

CI Divers & Pieter's Place

DIVE CENTRE

- 🐾 Accommodation and a dive centre; also has a large pool for training
- 🐾 Boats are launched 1km away and divers are taken there by car.

DIVES

Single or double tank: Both, as requested by divers

Divers per group: Usually four, maximum eight

Leaders per group: One dive leader

Centre to launch: 1km by car

Boat ride to dive sites: 10–30 mins

End of dive policy: Experienced divers can ascend as buddy pairs; inexperienced divers stay with the group. Dives are usually long, as 15-litre cylinders are used.

Main attractions: A very lovely wall runs from 12–120m depth, with large fan corals and diverse life, including turtles, sunfish, large groupers, kingfish and big schools of batfish.

BOATS

- 🐾 1 x 5m fibreglass boat
- 🐾 1 x 7m fibreglass boat
- 🐾 Oxygen on all dive trips

ACCOMMODATION

Small, quiet, relaxed. A basic family resort built around an enormous baobab tree, 100m from the beach. There are also self-catering units. Restaurant specialises in seafood. Pool table, darts, games, large-screen televisions, safe parking, free Wi-Fi and Internet.

GENERAL

Comprises: Dive centre and resort

Website: www.pietersdiversplace.co.za

Email: cidiversmozambique@gmail.com

Nearest airport: Pemba (6km by road)

Operating since: 1996

Courses offered: All PADI courses, from beginner to DM

Pemba Beach

Pieter's baobab

WHEN TO GO	Sea temp	Wind/rain	Good vis	Whales	Dolphins	Nudibranchs
Jan	28°C	✔	✔		✔	✔
Feb	27°C	✔	✔		✔	✔
Mar	26°C	✔	✔		✔	✔
Apr	26°C		✔		✔	✔
May	25°C		✔		✔	✔
Jun	25°C		✔		✔	✔
Jul	24°C		✔		✔	✔
Aug	25°C		✔	✔	✔	✔
Sep	26°C		✔	✔	✔	✔
Oct	26°C		✔	✔	✔	✔
Nov	27°C	✔	✔	✔	✔	✔
Dec	28°C	✔	✔		✔	✔

Note: Whale sharks and sharks are seldom encountered.

WHAT THEY SAY

We give good personal service and offer great diving, as well as snorkelling trips, whale and dolphin trips, mangrove trips and kayaking.

WHAT WE SAY

Pieter, who set up his dive centre in 1996, pioneered diving in the Pemba area and discovered most of the best-known sites here himself. Other people have come and gone, and at the time of writing Pieter's is the only dive centre in Pemba. Big cylinders and small groups mean long, peaceful dives. His knowledge of the sites is unsurpassed, and you know you are in good hands when out diving with him. The dive side of the business is known as CI Divers, while the accommodation is known as Pieter's Place.

The resort is built around a baobab tree that is believed to be about 1,000 years old and has a staircase built into it. The accommodation is simple but comfortable, with hot showers, private bathrooms and the essential air conditioning, backed up by a generator when necessary. There is free, reliable Wi-Fi. The kitchen and bar are open from 07h00 to 21h30. Try the home-made samosas, fish rissoles and prawns.

If you want more upscale accommodation look at the nearby Avani Pemba Beach Hotel and Spa and then book your dives with Pieter.

DIVE SITE INFORMATION

Pieter's top three dive sites are Finger North East (advanced divers only), The Gap (also advanced divers only) and The Turtle (suitable for all divers). The Turtle ranges from 5–18m, has lots of coral, few currents and is perfect for photographers and inexperienced divers. Sea horses, paper leaffish, lionfish and many other interesting fish can be seen.

Leaf fish *Taenianotus triacanthus*; this species comes in many different colours.

Dive #: 498   **Date:** 23rd May   **Dive Site:** Tunnel in the Wall
                                                                       Rated: 4

Vis stunning. Multiple colours and species of fish. A big turtle and one huge batfish, then a huge, serene school of around 100 batfish. Tunnel at about 38m; absolutely lovely.

Dive #: 500   **Date:** 31st May   **Dive Site:** Baobab Gardens
                                                                       Rated: 3

Beautiful site. Vis clear. Fish and corals colourful and varied. No need to go any deeper than 6m. A perfect dive for beginners. Very easy, relaxing, rewarding.

Dive #: 501   **Date:** 7th June   **Dive Site:** Reef slightly north of Londo
                                                                       Rated: 3

This was a pleasure: I just donned my gear, took the boat a couple of minutes out in front of Londo and dived in. Felt safe and happy and explored for 52 minutes. Saw another blue ribbon eel and two stingrays. A heavenly dive.

Dive #: 507   **Date:** 22nd June   **Dive Site:** Baobab Rocks
                                                                       Rated: 3

Loved this dive – so very calm and beautiful. Two magnificent lionfish on an old piece of chain; almost put my hand on one trying to free the chain from coral boulders. Then discovered a lovely snowflake moray on the same chain. Also found a tiny needlefish, with a head like a sea horse.

Dive #: 509   **Date:** 23rd June   **Dive Site:** Wall (advanced; deep)
                                                                       Rated: 3

This was a great dive – wall goes down and down forever. Very beautiful and serene.

Dive #: 510   **Date:** 23rd June   **Dive Site:** Shallows
                                                                       Rated: 3

Found my very first leaffish – bright yellow. Also saw an amazing multicoloured fish – not sure what – then two needlefish, a gorgeous blue-and-green boxfish and a black-and-gold one.

Dive #: 514   **Date:** 7th July   **Dive Site:** The Finger (with Pieter)
                                                                       Rated: 5

A truly fabulous dive site. Dropped down to about 25m and then swam over a wall to an endless drop (going down to 120m). Like flying. I went down to 42m and still couldn't see the bottom. Lovely snappers and fusiliers, bright blue and yellow, and a biiig Napoleon! On the way back we stopped and swam with wild dolphins – about four of them, just 2m away from me. Could even see their spots.

Dive #: 516   **Date:** 10th July   **Dive Site:** Middle of Pemba Bay
Rated: 3

We were out trying to locate new reefs, when we saw dolphins in the middle of the bay.

While we were trying to decide whether to dive with them, I suddenly saw an enormous shape breaking the surface, about 3m from the boat. At first I thought it was a great white, but then Ross said 'Sunfish!'

We scrambled into our gear, but by then it was gone. I went in anyway in the hope of seeing either the sunfish or the dolphins – but no luck. However, there were an astonishing number of large brown jellyfish; it looked like the jellyfish lake in Palau. They had long tentacles, so I tried to keep clear of them, but it wasn't easy finding the space to swim between them. Thank heavens for my wetsuit.

Dive #: 517   **Date:** 17th July   **Dive Site:** The Finger
Rated: 3

As glorious as the last time I dived it. Very big Napoleon swam with us for much of the way and when I turned away from it to see what Pieter was trying to show me, it followed me, bless its curious and friendly heart.

Dive #: 774   **Date:** 2nd June 2016   **Dive Site:** The Tunnel (The Gap) Pemba
Temp: 27°C   **Time:** 60 mins   **Depth:** 38m   **Rated:** 4

Just me and Pieter. Such a pleasure to launch gently in the flat bay. Warm, clear water. We dropped down through the blue to the tunnel at 38m. Very peaceful, with virtually no current. Lovely to look through the tunnel to the blue on the other side. Glided gently through, and then took our time exploring at depth, while we slowly made our way up again. We both went into deco and needed a prolonged safety stop, which suited me fine as I was enjoying all the beauty around me. Batfish, surgeonfish, baby Napoleon, nudis, schools of Moorish idols, green paper leaffish, beautiful gorgonian fans, colourful hard and soft corals, two big, beautiful cowries. Great topography, always interesting.

Dive #: 775   **Date:** 3rd June 2016   **Dive Site:** Finger North East (with CI Divers)
Temp: 27°C   **Time:** 62 mins   **Depth:** 30m   **Rated:** 4

Just Pieter and me again. Another beautiful day. Puttered out for about 15 minutes then dropped down, seemingly into the middle of nowhere. Negative descent – Pieter won't use an anchor here as there is no sand and he doesn't want to damage the corals. Dropped straight down to 30m. We found ourselves in a landscape of cabbage corals, on the edge of a seemingly endless drop; Pieter reckons between 60 and 120m in places. Expansive gorgonian fans everywhere. We swam around the edge of the drop till we reached 10 minutes deco time and then slowly swam to a shallower area. The next 40 minutes was a ramble through colour and beauty. The usual Indian Ocean suspects in all their glory. I saw my first yellow papillae flatworm, looking like a starry, starry night, with bright yellow spots on a black background and undulating edges. A strikingly lovely bright yellow trumpetfish, with its grey mate at its side; also angelfish, butterflyfish, boxfish, surgeonfish, big schools of fusiliers, Moorish idols, big-eyed soldierfish, crescent-tail bigeyes and squirrelfish. Really lovely dive.

Bushy black coral *Antipathes* sp.
Photo: Dennis King

Nampula
Province

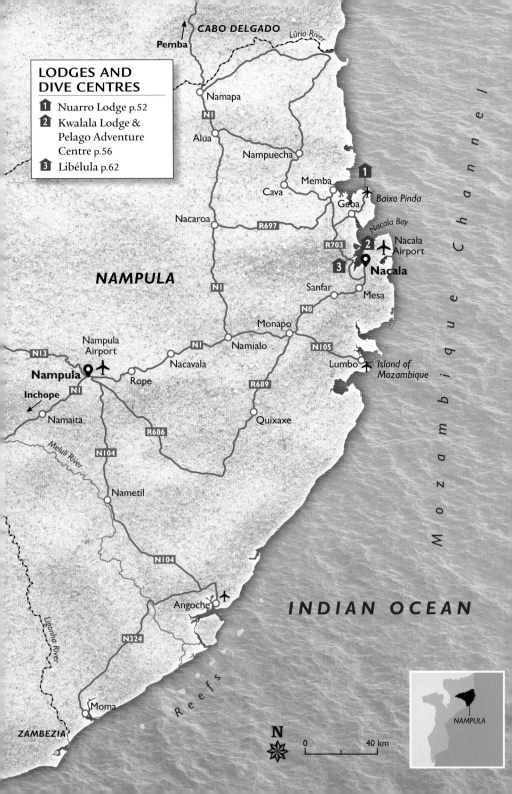

CABO DELGADO

Pemba

Lúrio River

LODGES AND DIVE CENTRES

1 Nuarro Lodge p.52
2 Kwalala Lodge & Pelago Adventure Centre p.56
3 Libélula p.62

Namapa

N1

Alua

Nampuecha

Memba

Cava

Geba

1

Baixo Pinda

Nacala Bay

Nacaroa

R697

R703

2

Nacala Airport

3

Nacala

NAMPULA

Sanfar

Mesa

N1

N8

Monapo

Nampula Airport

N1

Namialo

N105

N13

Nacavala

Lumbo

Island of Mozambique

Nampula

Rope

R689

Inchope

N1

Namaita

Quixaxe

R686

Meluli River

N104

Nametil

N104

Ligonha River

N324

Angoche

INDIAN OCEAN

Moma

ZAMBEZIA

N

0   40 km

Reefs

M o z a m b i q u e   C h a n n e l

NAMPULA

Nampula Province lies to the south of Cabo Delgado Province. It is popular with divers who prefer to avoid surf entries, as most of the diving is in a quiet bay. There is also easy access for shore diving, which is not the norm in Mozambique.

You can enjoy wall dives with huge gorgonians, unexplored reefs, calm waters, a high diversity of fish and invertebrates and even whales in season. However, sightings of dolphins, mantas and sharks, including whale sharks, are rare in this area.

Of all the diving locations in Mozambique, Nampula seems to have the most extraordinary collection of unusual fish. (Read the dive log extracts to get an idea of a dive here – there's nothing typical about Nampula diving!)

The resorts are relatively quiet, with an emphasis on personalised service. The World Heritage Site Ilha de Mozambique is around two hours from Nacala Bay, on the northern coast of Mozambique, and makes an interesting day trip.

As the province is quite near the equator, the weather is always warm, and the sea temperature varies between 26 and 28°C.

The following table provides some guidance on the best times to visit the area, but you should also check the information supplied for the individual dive resorts.

Anemone with skunk anemonefish *Amphiprion akallopisos*

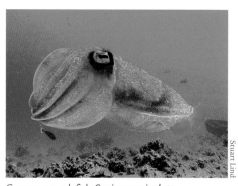

Common cuttlefish *Sepia vermiculata*

WHEN TO VISIT	Sea temp	Wind/rain	Good vis	Whales	Nudibranchs
Jan	25–30°C	✔			✔
Feb	25–30°C	✔			✔
Mar	25–30°C	✔			✔
Apr	23–28°C				✔
May	23–28°C		✔		✔
Jun	21–26°C		✔	✔	✔
Jul	21–26°C		✔	✔	✔
Aug	22–27°C		✔	✔	✔
Sep	23–28°C		✔	✔	✔
Oct	25–30°C		✔	✔	✔
Nov	25–30°C		✔	✔	✔
Dec	25–30°C	✔	✔		✔

Nuarro Lodge

DIVE CENTRE

🐾 Tea and coffee, hot showers, nitrox available

🐾 Staff will assist with the gear, set up, wash and put away, unless you prefer to do it

🐾 Towels and water provided on boats

DIVES

Single or double tank: As requested
Divers per group: 1–6
DMs per group: 1–2
Centre to launch: Directly from centre
Boat ride to dive sites: 2–20 mins
End of dive policy: Depends on divers' qualifications
Main attractions: Great visibility year-round, beautiful wall dives with huge gorgonians, calm waters, unexplored tropical reefs with a high diversity of fish and invertebrates, whales approaching close to shore in blue water, shore dives and night dives. No surf entries, easy launches and easy boat rides. The calm water and exclusivity of the diving make Nuarro highly suitable for underwater photographers, particularly macro photographers.

BOATS

🐾 1 x 6.5m RIB with 2 x 60 h.p. 4-stroke motors

🐾 1 x 5m skiff with 40 h.p. motor

🐾 Full complement of safety equipment on board, including oxygen and radios

Loading the boat for a dive

The shy blackspotted puffer *Arothron nigropunctatus* is usually seen alone.

Aerial picture of Baixo do Pinda clearly showing the different depths of the water

The restaurant at night

One of the chalets

Kayaking in the mangroves

ACCOMMODATION

A luxury eco-resort on the dunes – quiet, peaceful and suitable for families. Offers snorkelling, massages, mountain biking, kayaking, picnics and mangrove and village visits.

GENERAL

Comprises: Resort with dive centre
Website: www.nuarro.com
Email: reservations@nuarro.com
Nearest airport: Nacala; then 85km (two hours) by car or a private plane charter from Nacala, Nampula or Pemba to Nuarro Lodge's registered airstrip
Operating since: 2009
Courses offered: PADI

WHEN TO GO	Sea temp	Wind/rain	Good vis	Whales	Nudibranchs
Jan	30°C	✔	✔		✔
Feb	30°C	✔	✔		✔
Mar	30°C	✔	✔		✔
Apr	28°C		✔		✔
May	28°C		✔		✔
Jun	27°C		✔		✔
Jul	26°C		✔	✔	✔
Aug	25°C		✔	✔	✔
Sep	26°C		✔	✔	✔
Oct	27°C		✔	✔	✔
Nov	28–29°C		✔		✔
Dec	29–30°C		✔		✔

Note: Nuarro Lodge is closed from January to mid-March for international bookings.

WHAT THEY SAY

Location is everything. Nuarro is the only lodge in Mozambique where you can dive from the shore directly onto a huge wall. We sit on the edge of the continental shelf, which makes for outstanding diving.

WHAT WE SAY

Please note that we have not yet dived with Nuarro.

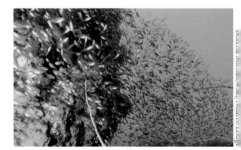

The wall

Bryde's whales *Balaenoptera brydei* in the bay

Yara Tibiriçá

Thorny sea horse *Hippocampus histrix*

Kwalala Lodge & Pelago Adventure Centre

DIVE CENTRE

🐾 Kit is transferred to and from the boat by the staff, then washed and packed away

🐾 Tea, coffee, cool drinks, water available

🐾 No nitrox

DIVES

Single or double tank: As requested

Divers per group: 2–8

Leaders per group: One

Centre to launch: Launch from directly in front of centre

Boat ride to dive sites: 10–60 mins

Dive policy: In a group, or the buddy system for larger groups

End of dive policy: All divers dive to 50 bar

Daniel van Duinkerken

Colourful giant frogfish *Antennarius commerson*

Rob Koch

A starry moray *Gymnothorax nudivomer* hides in the sand.

A Discover Scuba Diving course gives you the chance to try diving for one day.

The stone chalets were built from local stone.

Stuart Lind

A passing dhow

Main attractions: The marine reserve offers excellent shore dives for all levels of diver. The resident bigeye kingfish school around the divers, while Indian Ocean walkman, stonefish, lionfish, leaffish, sea horses and giant pipefish are often seen, and there are little harlequin shrimps that live in the shallows. Outside the bay you can dive a big steamer shipwreck that sits at 17m. The wreck still has its old steamers, anchor and propeller. Close to the wreck there is a beautiful wall with plenty of hard and soft corals and big schools of fish. Nacala Bay is generally calm, so entries are smooth and, as the lodge is situated in the bay, it is possible to hide from any bad weather by choosing which side of the bay to dive.

BOATS

6 x single- and double-engine fibreglass boats

Oxygen on all trips

ACCOMMODATION

A quiet, comfortable family resort right on the shore of Nacala Bay. There are never more than 20 guests. Additional activities include snorkelling, kayaking, stand-up paddleboarding, whale-watching and picnics.

GENERAL

Comprises: Resort, dive centre and restaurant
Website: www.kwalala-lodges.com
Email: info@kwalala-lodges.com (lodge),
pelago@kwalala-lodges.com (dive manager)
Nearest airport: Nacala Airport when operational, then 10 mins by road; currently Nampula Airport, then 2.5 hours by road
Operating since: 2001
Courses offered: PADI

A diver on the wall at the gorgonian fan forest at Nangata

WHEN TO GO	Sea temp	Wind/rain	Good vis	Whales	Nudibranchs
Jan	25–30°C	✔		✔	✔
Feb	25–30°C	✔			✔
Mar	25–30°C	✔			✔
Apr	23–28°C		✔		✔
May	23–28°C		✔		✔
Jun	21–26°C		✔		✔
Jul	21–26°C		✔	✔	✔
Aug	22–27°C		✔	✔	✔
Sep	23–28°C		✔	✔	✔
Oct	25–30°C		✔	✔	✔
Nov	25–30°C		✔	✔	✔
Dec	25–30°C	✔	✔	✔	✔

Note: It is rainy from December to March.

WHAT THEY SAY

Our dive instructors have extensive knowledge of the Nacala Bay area. We consider dive safety a high priority and all our compressors and dive equipment are regularly serviced and inspected. We are also flexible and will tailor-make a diving adventure for you or your group. As we do not have a large number of divers we can give all our attention to our divers.

WHAT WE SAY

Mike and Shirley Donald have lovingly built Kwalala out of beautiful stone over the past 10 years. There is comfortable accommodation (Kwalala Lodge), a dive centre (Pelago Adventures) and a restaurant overlooking the sea (The Thirsty Whale).

The Thirsty Whale offers breakfast all day, and their breakfast muffins and chocolate cake are a must.

At the time of publishing, the closest functioning airport to Nacala is Nampula. This necessitates a 2.5-hour road trip to Nacala. Resorts will send someone to fetch you, but everyone is looking forward to the day when the new airport at Nacala becomes international, enabling one to fly to within 8km of the resorts.

Arrowhead soapfish *Belonoperca chabanaudi*

Nudibranch *Ardeadoris* sp.

Dive #: 788   **Date:** 20th June 2016   **Dive Site:** Mike's Marathon, Kwalala House Reef
Temp: 26°C   **Time:** 48 mins   **Depth:** 41.3m   **Rated:** 4

Mike combined several dives (including Amy's Rock, Matthew's Castle, Gold Reef City and Bonito Rock) into one so that I could see as much as possible. This dive was such fun. I felt like a child in a playground – so much to see and such fun discovering the next surprise. Mike has had the area around the resort declared a conservation zone in an effort to save the reef. To help it recover its former beauty he has created false reefs all over, using 10 cars, wheelbarrows, building blocks and even an old dive platform. In just 10 years they have already started to accumulate a surprising abundance of coral and fish species.

Mantis shrimp

Stuart Lind

    Amazing that this is their house reef. I felt as if I had dived into a *National Geographic* special. Among other rarities, I saw four leaffish, an octopus and multiple mantis shrimps, beautiful whip corals, a nursery, a cleaning station, crayfish, bigeye trevallies, ribbon eels, emperor angelfish, boxfish and tuna.

Leaf fish

Stuart Lind

Dive #: 790   **Date:** 20th June 2016   **Dive Site:** Napala House Reef
Temp: 26°C   **Time:** 47 mins   **Depth:** 31.3m   **Rated:** 3

Dived straight down to a wall and enjoyed the dramatic topography of peaks and troughs. On the way up we encountered two juvenile emperor angelfish and the smallest toby I've ever seen. Another mantis shrimp, another ribbon eel, beautiful big blue boxfish with white spots. Mike almost touched a scorpionfish while he was trying to show me something. Two juvenile geometric morays. As we reached 5m we came to a grassed area covered with hundreds of starfish, of all colours and sizes, some really beautiful. A light blue one with bright yellow spots comes to mind. Somehow Mike spotted a crocodile snake eel in the long grass, just centimetres away from me, and we also saw a sand eel's head sticking out of the sand, his jaw opening and shutting. We slowly crept quite close to him, and he didn't seem to mind our presence at all.

Juvenile emperor angelfish

Rob Koch

Bannerfish, sea goldies and black pyramid butterflyfish

Stuart Lind

Dive #: 791   **Date:** 21st June 2016   **Dive Site:** Lighthouse Wall
Temp: 26°C   **Time:** 48 mins   **Depth:** 38m   **Rated:** 3

Went quite a long way across the bay for this dive but it was worth it. Exhilarating drop-off, followed by a slow ascent in world-class corals and an accompanying burst of the most colourful fish, including a new one for me. Variegated something, 5cm, brownish and cream, big fin above forehead. Just beauty everywhere.

Dive #: 792   **Date:** 21st June 2016   **Dive Site:** Nangata Wall
Temp: 26°C   **Time:** 39 mins   **Depth:** 35.5m   **Rated:** 4

Fabulous dive near Nuarro Lighthouse. An endless drop-off, with the biggest gorgonian fans I've ever seen – and they were everywhere. On the slow ascent we saw magnificent hard and soft corals and huge shoals of fish zooming up and down past us. Swirling blue-striped fusiliers. Hard to describe the abundance of this dive; sensory overload.

Bannerfish

Rob Koch

Dive #: 793   **Date:** 21st June 2016   **Dive Site:** Night Dive, Kwalala House Reef
Temp: 26°C   **Time:** 62 mins   **Depth:** 24m   **Rated:** 5

I hardly ever rate a dive a 5, but this one was truly astonishing. We walked in from the beach at night to find one surprise after another. Almost immediately it started – kingklip, catfish, tropical lobster. A beautiful tiger cowrie in its envelope. Hermit crabs everywhere, many with yellow-and-red bodies. Sponge spider crab, flathead crocodilefish. Electric rays hunting. Sleeping triggerfish. Multiple pipefish. There was more to come.

Ornate spiny lobster

Dennis King

While we were watching, a large green-headed moray suddenly uncurled itself and started hunting a big blue fish. With a lightning flash it struck its prey and took it back to its cave. There were two exquisitely mottled Spanish dancer-type nudibranchs (cream and brown, not orange and red). Both were swimming, furling and unfurling their skirts as they undulated through the water. Quite mesmerising. At one point I was admiring a large scorpionfish on the hood of one of the cars when I spotted a real Spanish dancer resting below. Next to the scorpionfish was a piece of coral on which were an adult and a juvenile leaffish, side by side. Two octopi, Natal dancing shrimps, which gave us a manicure, red-banded shrimp, cleaner shrimp and spiny lobsters.

All too soon Mike ended the dive – 62 minutes of spotlit enchantment.

DIVE CENTRE

🐾 Restaurant at the centre
🐾 Kayaks available
🐾 No nitrox
🐾 Gear rinsed and stored by staff

DIVES

Single or double tank: As requested by divers
Divers per group: Maximum of five
DMs per group: One
Centre to launch: Directly from centre
Boat ride to dive sites: 25–30 mins
End of dive policy: They try to make sure that each diver gets to stay down until he or she reaches 50 bar.
Main attractions: A thriving unofficial marine reserve for the past 10 years, boasting macro life, leaffish, scorpionfish, stonefish, ribbon eels, moray eels, sea horses, nudibranchs and, occasionally, octopus.

Ornate ghost pipefish *Solenostomus paradoxus*

The yellow-mouth moray *Gymnothorax nudivomer* and humpback cleaner shrimp *Lysmata amboinensis* have a symbiotic relationship – the shrimp cleans the moray's teeth, thereby gaining a meal.

The coral rockcod *Cephalopholis miniata* is a bright orange-red; juveniles have blue spots.

BOATS

🐟 1 x fibreglass boat with 15 h.p. engine
🐟 Towels and water provided on boats
🐟 Oxygen on all dive trips

ACCOMMODATION

A quiet, peaceful, mid-range family resort with a restaurant and swimming pool. It is built on an escarpment. A 100-step staircase leads down to the beach below.

Ian Kingsley

Sunset at the restaurant

WHEN TO GO	Sea temp	Wind/rain	Good vis	Whales	Nudibranchs
Jan	26°C	✔			✔
Feb	27°C	✔			✔
Mar	27°C	✔			✔
Apr	26°C	✔			✔
May	25°C		✔		✔
Jun	23°C		✔		✔
Jul	23°C		✔		✔
Aug	22°C	✔	✔	✔	✔
Sep	22°C		✔	✔	✔
Oct	22°C			✔	✔
Nov	24°C				✔
Dec	25°C				✔

Nudibranch *Hypselodoris pulchella*

GENERAL

Comprises: Resort with dive centre
Website: www.divelibelula.com
Email: info@divelibelula.com
Nearest airport: Nacala Airport (when open), then 3km by car; otherwise two hours' drive from Nampula Airport
Operating since: 2009
Courses offered: PADI Advanced

WHAT THEY SAY

We offer a relaxing environment, personal service, a beautiful beach and great food. We are close to the airport (when Nacala is open). Easy access to shore dives means no walks carrying gear. Everything is right on the beach.

EXTRACTS FROM ROBYNN'S DIVE LOG

Dive #: 794	Date: 22nd June 2016		Dive Site: Libelula House Reef
Temp: 26°C	58 mins	Depth: 30m	Rated: 4

Quite absurd to think that this reef is at the bottom of Ian and PJ's garden. We walked in from the beach and after about 30m of swimming came across a beautiful bommie, complete with goldies, chromis, coachmen, juvenile emperor angelfish and many others. The dive continued in this way – bommies interspersed with sand. In the sand we found three sea horses and about five pipefish. Normally any one of these would be the highlight of a dive, but this is just everyday diving at Nacala. Scorpionfish galore: a special moment for me was a piece of coral with two tiny juveniles. Tobies everywhere. Four juvenile emperor angelfish – the most I've ever seen on a single dive. Two shoals of bannerfish. Three leaffish.

Dive #: 795	Date: 23rd June 2016		Dive Site: Napala Dropoff
Temp: 26°C	Time: 52 mins	Depth: 32m	Rated: 3

We dropped down a wall to 32m and then spent the rest of the dive slowly ascending as we took in the lovely corals. All the usual Indian Ocean fish were there in abundance. I remember in particular a yellow leaffish. There was also a fish I haven't seen before and can't identify. It was shaped like an ordinary damsel, perhaps 13cm long. Its colours were the interesting part: blues, pinks and mauves all 'water-coloured' into each other. The most identifiable feature was the anal fin, which had bright orange markings.

The end of the dive was spectacular: we came upon huge bommies of bubble coral, forming a backdrop for thousands of brightly coloured fish, including goldies, chromis and antheas. As we were only about 7m deep, the sun sparkled off the bubbles and the fish, creating a fairyland of colour.

WHAT WE SAY

Ian and PJ have created a laid-back haven here. The garden cottages, main house, restaurant and pool area blend well with the naturally beautiful tropical setting. To get to the beach you walk down a flight of 100 stone steps winding through the trees. All dive gear is kept in a beach house, so you can kit up there.

The cottage where we stayed had two bedrooms, a bathroom with shower and bath, an open-plan kitchen and a living area. All the rooms have fans and air conditioning and the windows are netted, so mosquitoes are not a problem.

The main drawcard here is the weird and wonderful creatures seen on dives. There is something exotic around every corner.

Ian Kingsley

Sea horse *Hippocampus fuscus*

A diver can pause in a spot like this and witness a whole new world.

This remora fish has attached itself to a leopard shark. The remora feeds on parasites taken from the shark's skin and mouth, and thus both species benefit from the relationship.

Photo: Daniel van Duinkerken

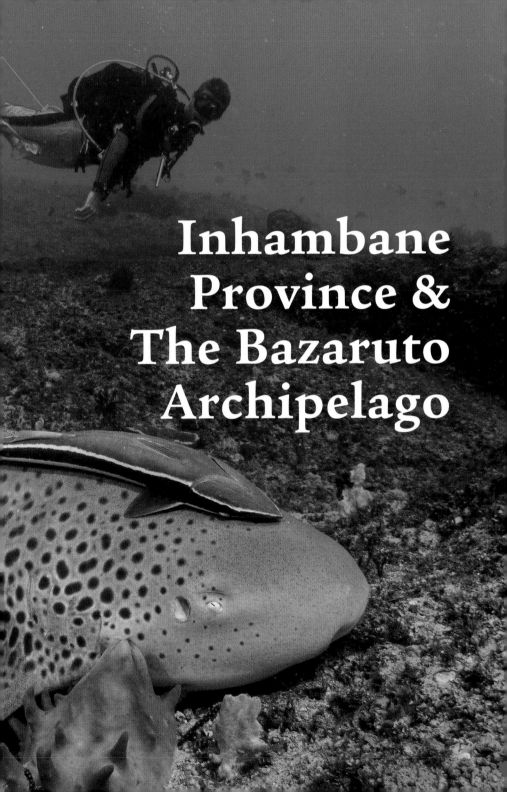

Inhambane Province & The Bazaruto Archipelago

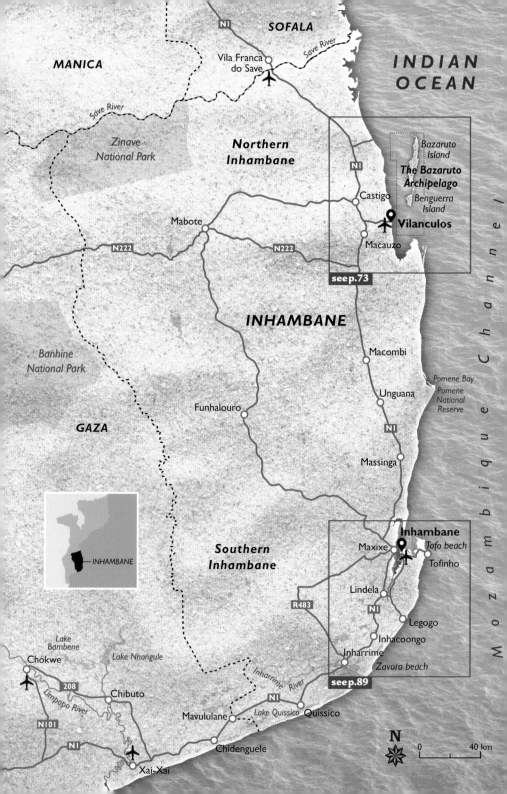

MANICA

SOFALA

N1

Vila Franca
do Save

Save River

INDIAN
OCEAN

Save River

Zinave
National Park

Northern
Inhambane

Bazaruto
Island

The Bazaruto
Archipelago

N1

Castigo

Benguerra
Island

Mabote

Vilanculos

N222

N222

Macauzo

see p.73

INHAMBANE

Banhine
National Park

Macombi

Unguana

Pomene Bay

Pomene
National
Reserve

Funhalouro

GAZA

N1

Massinga

INHAMBANE

Inhambane

Tofo beach

Maxixe

Tofinho

Southern
Inhambane

Lindela

N1

R483

Legogo

Inhacoongo

Lake
Bambene

Lake Nhangule

Inharrime

Zavora beach

Chókwe

Chibuto

Inharrime River

see p.89

Limpopo River

208

Mavululane

Lake Quissico

Quissico

N1

N101

N1

Chidenguele

Xai-Xai

N

0   40 km

Mozambique Channel

The whale shark *Rhincodon typus* is the biggest fish on the planet. These gentle giants can reach 12m in length and live for more than 70 years.

The diving varies considerably along Inhambane's extensive coastline, so make sure that you plan very carefully and choose the correct time and place to see the creatures you're interested in. **Do not assume that information given for one Inhambane dive resort necessarily applies to the others.** The table below will guide you on the best times to visit the area, but for more specific information, check the tables and descriptions given for the individual resorts and dive centres.

The resorts in Inhambane and the Bazaruto Archipelago are also diverse, ranging from informal and beachy to luxurious and exclusive, so use the resort information given in the text in combination with the resort's website to determine the right one for you.

WHEN TO VISIT	Sea temp	Wind/ rain	Good vis	Whales	Whale sharks	Dolphins	Mantas	Sharks	Nudibranchs
Jan	28°C					✔	✔	✔	✔
Feb	28°C	✔				✔	✔	✔	✔
Mar	28°C					✔	✔	✔	✔
Apr	27°C	✔				✔	✔	✔	✔
May	26°C	✔				✔	✔	✔	✔
Jun	25°C	✔	✔			✔	✔	✔	✔
Jul	21°C	✔	✔			✔	✔	✔	✔
Aug	22°C	✔	✔	✔	✔	✔	✔	✔	✔
Sep	26°C	✔	✔	✔	✔	✔	✔	✔	✔
Oct	27°C	✔	✔	✔	✔	✔	✔	✔	✔
Nov	27°C	✔			✔	✔	✔	✔	✔
Dec	28°C				✔	✔	✔	✔	✔

Note: July and August are peak season for whales, while October to December are prime months for mantas.

Inhambane is world-famous for its large pelagics, especially manta rays, humpback whales and whale sharks. There are also turtles, game fish, devil rays, sharks and fascinating macro life.

Humpback whales pass through the area from June to October, as they migrate from the South Pole to the warmer waters of the Indian Ocean to give birth. Manta rays are seen year-round in some, but not all, areas.

Off Tofo, 'Whale Shark Alley' (a plankton-rich corridor) attracts whale sharks. Although they typically occur here later in the year, this is variable: in March 2017, 12 were sighted at Tofo on one day.

Most resorts offer boat trips for viewing whale sharks. When the sharks are sighted, snorkellers drop quietly off the boat at a respectful distance and watch as the peaceful giants swim by. This is an experience not to be missed.

The Bazaruto Archipelago, comprising six islands, has been declared a national park. It covers 1,400km² and has pristine coral reefs,

Colourful life on a coral bommie

The magnificent honeycomb moray *Gymnothorax favagineus*. Behind the sharp, backward-pointing teeth is another complete set of jaws, which can project forward to grasp prey.

An aerial view of the Bazaruto Archipelago

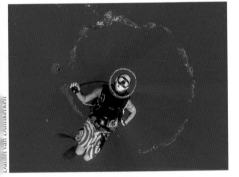

A diver blows expanding bubbles on a safety stop.

with whales, dolphins and more than 2,000 species of fish.

There are luxury dive resorts on Bazaruto and Benguerra islands, set amid breathtaking scenic beauty.

On the mainland, from Vilanculos to Zavora, a coastline of about 400km, the diving is characterised by:

🐾 pristine dive sites
🐾 beautiful corals, and
🐾 marine life that embraces the smallest nudibranchs to the biggest mantas, whales, whales sharks and dugongs.

Around Vilanculos dive conditions are quiet and easy. The Bazaruto Archipelago boasts incredible scenery, while Pomene and Zavora are known for their beautiful beaches. Moreover, both Inhambane and the Bazaruto Archipelago enjoy a warm tropical climate and a sea temperature of between 22 and 28°C.

Note that given the vast distances being covered, we have divided this section into two parts: northern (p.72) and southern (p.88).

It is an immense privilege to swim with whale sharks *Rhincodon typus*. Even when divers keep a respectful distance, these curious and friendly creatures often swim closer.

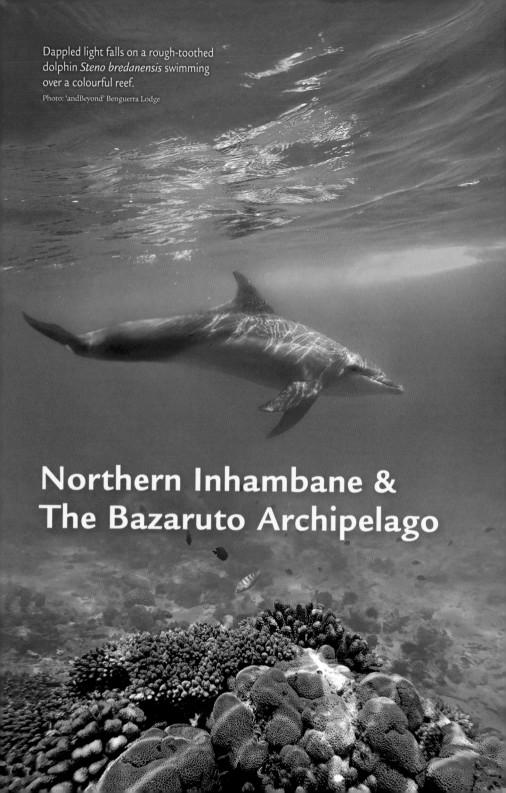

Dappled light falls on a rough-toothed dolphin *Steno bredanensis* swimming over a colourful reef.
Photo: 'andBeyond' Benguerra Lodge

Northern Inhambane & The Bazaruto Archipelago

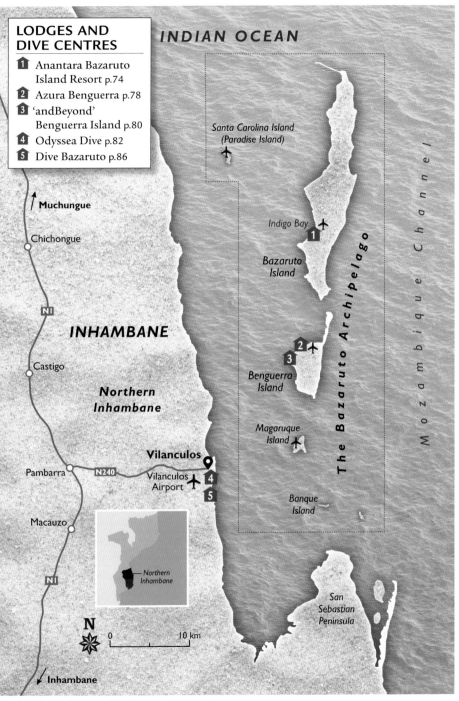

LODGES AND DIVE CENTRES

1 Anantara Bazaruto
Island Resort p.74

2 Azura Benguerra p.78

3 'andBeyond'
Benguerra Island p.80

4 Odyssea Dive p.82

5 Dive Bazaruto p.86

INDIAN OCEAN

Santa Carolina Island
(Paradise Island)

Muchungue

Chichongue

Indigo Bay

1

Bazaruto
Island

Mozambique Channel

NI

INHAMBANE

The Bazaruto Archipelago

Castigo

2

3

Benguerra
Island

Northern
Inhambane

Magaruque
Island

Vilanculos

Pambarra   N240   Vilanculos   **4**
Airport   **5**

Banque
Island

Macauzo

Northern
Inhambane

NI

San
Sebastian
Peninsula

N

0   10 km

Inhambane

Northern Inhambane and The Bazaruto Archipelago

Anantara Bazaruto Island Resort

DIVE CENTRE

🐾 High-quality dive gear is supplied free of charge

🐾 If you use your own gear, it is rinsed and stored for you

🐾 Staff set up gear

🐾 10- and 12-litre steel cylinders (depending on guest preference and air consumption)

🐾 Dive computers available for hire

DIVES

Single or double tank: As requested
Divers per group: 1–8
Leaders per group: PADI instructor leads all groups
Centre to launch: Boats launch directly from dive centre
Boat ride to dive sites: 10–45 mins

End of dive policy: Everyone dives till they reach 50 bar; divers using up their air faster wait on the boat.

Main attractions: Over 100 species of coral, thousands of tropical fish species, five kinds of dolphin, four whale and shark species, all five marine turtle species and the largest population of dugongs on the African east coast.

From the age of eight, children can learn to dive with PADI's Bubblemaker course.

The main building at Anantara Bazaruto; the adventure sand dunes are visible in the background.

Fish flashing past in a burst of colour

BOATS

🐟 1 x 31ft fibreglass Gulf Craft with
2 x 175 h.p. Suzuki outboards, GPS and
marine VHF (very high frequency)
🐟 DAN oxygen kits on all boats

ACCOMMODATION

A luxury, family-friendly resort; the beach
villas are 20m from the water, while the
deluxe sea-view pool villas are set up on
the hill, with paths leading to the main guest
areas and beach.

EXTRACT FROM
ROBYNN'S TRAVEL LOG

Indigo Bay is serene and quite breathtakingly
beautiful.

All of the chalets have sea views. Some
are literally on the beach, while others are
slightly higher up, with private swimming
pools and decks overlooking the ocean. It
is so quiet that one's ears ring.

Every luxury and practicality that you can
think of has been provided, from three types
of electrical plug to satin sheets and soft
pillows. In addition to a private swimming
pool, my house had both an indoor and an
outdoor shower, a lovely oval bath in the
main bedroom, televisions and telephones
in every room and another en-suite wing I
didn't even need.

This is the ideal resort for divers travelling
with non-diving partners. There is so much
for them to do.

One of the highlights of my visit was
an exhilarating horse ride. I asked for the
advanced ride and I got it, cantering fast
along sandy paths up to the dunes, a climb
to the very top of the highest dune, followed
by a hair-raising descent. The horses are
brilliant, stepping thigh-deep into the sand,
and taking their charges safely back to the
sandy paths and home.

Horseriding along the beach and up the steep dunes is an added attraction.

GENERAL

Comprises: Luxury resort with its own dive centre

Web: www.bazaruto.anantara.com (part of Minor Hotels www.minorhotels.com)

Nearest airport: Vilanculos

Operating since: 2001

Courses offered: A PADI instructor is permanently based at the resort to teach all levels.

WHEN TO GO

The diving is good year-round, but most spectacular from April to November.

WHAT THEY SAY

Anantara Bazaruto Island Resort is sheer modern luxury. There is fishing, horseback riding, duneboarding, snorkelling, windsurfing, stand-up paddleboarding, kayaking and water-skiing. The diving is world class. There is a beautiful spa with incredible ocean views.

WHAT WE SAY

From the moment the private plane flies over the azure waters surrounding Bazaruto Island, you know are going somewhere different, somewhere special. (See extract from travel log, p.75.)

EXTRACTS FROM ROBYNN'S DIVE LOG

Dive #: 538   **Date:** 21st September   **Dive Site:** Two-Mile Reef

Rated: 5

Sheena (from England) and I were the only divers aboard the comfortable Gulf Craft. A windless, blue-sky day.

The trip out to Two-Mile Reef was flat and easy and took about 20 minutes. In a quiet bay we kitted up and then drove the eight minutes to the drop-off site. The DM led us around — there was beauty and colour everywhere.

Suddenly I saw the shine of a devil ray's wings. It was coming straight towards us, and behind it were about six more. We floated, enchanted as they played around us, completely unafraid and seemingly curious. Magical moment.

Later we found a big turtle unconcernedly eating bits vegetation from a rock. It remained completely relaxed as I sank down quietly next to it and watched.

While we were watching a large shoal of brightly coloured surgeonfish, I suddenly saw a shark swimming determinedly past. Apparently it was a bullshark! Later we saw the massive turtle we'd seen on the previous dive, still sleeping in his cave, then later an even bigger turtle. Just enormous — easily the biggest I've ever seen.
Fabulous dive.

Bluebanded surgeonfish

A diver photographs a small-eyed stingray *Dasyatis microps*. This species tends to grow very large.

Azura Benguerra

DIVE CENTRE

- The dive centre is located next to the restaurant, in the middle of the resort.
- Staff set up gear, load it onto and off the boat, and rinse it.
- PADI five-star resort with complete Scubapro equipment
- Both PADI MSDT instructors are Scubapro-certified technicians.

DIVES

Single or double tank: As requested
Divers per group: Usually 2–4, maximum six
DMs per group: One
Centre to launch: Directly in front of dive centre
Boat ride to dive sites: 25–75 mins
Dive policy: Divers have to stay with the group
End of dive policy: Varies
Main attractions: The reefs of the Bazaruto Archipelago are famous for their varied hard and soft corals and the diversity of their reef and pelagic species. Here there are regular sightings of loggerhead, green and hawksbill turtles, as well as a variety of reef shark species. On occasion dugongs are sighted at the surface; more rarely they are seen underwater on Two-Mile Reef.

BOATS

- 1 x 24ft Nova Cat catamaran powered by 2 x 150 h.p. Yamaha 4-stroke engines
- Towels, refreshments and snacks provided
- Oxygen on all boats

A longfin batfish *Platax teira* surprises a diver.

The villas are located right on the beach.

WHEN TO GO	Sea temp	Wind/ rain	Good vis	Whales	Whale sharks	Dolphins	Mantas	Sharks	Nudibranchs
Jan	28°C				✔	✔	✔	✔	✔
Feb	28°C	✔				✔	✔	✔	✔
Mar	28°C					✔	✔	✔	✔
Apr	27°C	✔				✔	✔	✔	✔
May	26°C	✔				✔	✔	✔	✔
Jun	25°C	✔	✔			✔	✔	✔	✔
Jul	24°C	✔	✔			✔	✔	✔	✔
Aug	24°C	✔	✔	✔	✔	✔	✔	✔	✔
Sep	26°C	✔	✔	✔		✔	✔	✔	✔
Oct	27°C	✔	✔	✔	✔	✔	✔	✔	✔
Nov	27°C	✔			✔	✔	✔	✔	✔
Dec	28°C				✔	✔	✔	✔	✔

Note: July and August are excellent months for viewing whales, although there is still a good chance of seeing them in September, and a slight chance in June and October. The prime months for seeing mantas are October to December.

ACCOMMODATION

Each villa has been designed with seclusion in mind. Just footsteps from the beach, they are a haven of rest and relaxation, where guests can feel at one with the environment. Activities available at the resort include snorkelling, fishing, island drives, sunset dhow cruises, picnics and day trips to other islands.

Azura Benguerra Infinity Beach villa

GENERAL

Comprises: A retreat that has its own dive centre
Website: www.azura-retreats.com
Email: reservations@azura-retreats.com
Where: Benguerra Island
Nearest airport: Vilanculos; then 7 mins by helicopter to the island
Operating since: October 2007
Courses offered: All PADI courses from Bubblemaker to Advanced Open Water

WHAT THEY SAY

We offer a five-star experience, where we take care of your every need so that you can relax and enjoy the beautiful diving that Mozambique has to offer. Our staff are well trained in making your trip as comfortable and enjoyable as possible. Our fully kitted five-star PADI dive centre has the latest Scubapro equipment for you to use.

WHAT WE SAY

We have not yet dived with Azura Benguerra.

'andBeyond'
Benguerra Island

DIVE CENTRE
On the beach

DIVES
Single or double tank: As requested
Divers per group: Not more than four
Leaders per group: One instructor or DM
Centre to launch: Directly from resort

Loading the Catamaran

Boat ride to dive sites: 30–40 mins
End of dive policy: Agreed prior to each dive
Main attractions: Plentiful fish life, great coral
and a good chance to encounter large fish.
Marlin may be seen in October.

BOATS
4 x 8m Catamarans each with 2 x Yamaha
outboards
1 x RIB with Suzuki 90 h.p. for diving and
snorkelling
1 x 12m Catamaran with 2 x Suzuki
outboards
Oxygen on all boats

ACCOMMODATION
The luxury resort is quiet and peaceful.
Activities include snorkelling, island hopping,
massages and picnics.

Yachts anchored in the bay in front of the resort

WHEN TO GO	Sea temp	Wind/ rain	Good vis	Whales	Dolphins	Mantas	Sharks	Nudibranchs
Jan	29°C	✔			✔	✔	✔	✔
Feb	29°C	✔			✔	✔	✔	✔
Mar	28°C				✔	✔	✔	✔
Apr	27°C				✔	✔	✔	✔
May	26°C		✔		✔	✔	✔	✔
Jun	25°C		✔		✔	✔	✔	✔
Jul	24°C		✔	✔	✔	✔	✔	✔
Aug	25°C		✔	✔	✔	✔	✔	✔
Sep	25°C			✔	✔	✔	✔	✔
Oct	28°C			✔	✔	✔	✔	✔
Nov	28°C				✔	✔	✔	✔
Dec	29°C				✔	✔	✔	✔

Note: Whale sharks are sometimes encountered.

GENERAL

Comprises: Lodge and dive centre
Website: www.andbeyond.com
Email: contactus@andBeyond.com
Nearest airport: Vilanculos; then 10 mins' helicopter flight directly to lodge
Operating since: 1990; under 'andBeyond' management since July 2015
Courses offered: PADI courses up to Divemaster

WHAT THEY SAY

We are a luxury resort catering to our guests' every wish. We dive in small groups to good dive sites and provide a professional and personal service.

WHAT WE SAY

Please note that we have not yet dived with 'andBeyond' Benguerra Lodge.

A diver watches a school of snappers and a goldbar wrasse *Thalassoma hebraicum*

Odyssea Dive

DIVE CENTRE

🐾 Showers, tea, coffee and home-made cake after dives

🐾 No nitrox

DIVES

Single or double tank: Usually double – a full-day trip including two dives, with a stopover on Bazaruto Island

Divers per group: Maximum of six

Leaders per group: One

Centre to launch: Directly from dive centre

Boat ride to dive sites: About 45 mins

End of dive policy: They do their best to give each diver their maximum dive time, up to 60 mins

Main attractions: Varied and colourful hard and soft corals, massive shoals of surgeonfish, every kind of trigger- and parrotfish, nudibranchs, honeycomb morays, mantas, devil rays, stingrays, lionfish, huge turtles, massive groupers, reef sharks, hammerheads, whale sharks, dugongs and humpbacks.

BOATS

🐾 1 x 8.5m hard-nose rubber duck, with two engines

🐾 Lunch and water provided

🐾 Oxygen on all trips

Nudibranch *Aegires minor*

A typically curious and friendly malabar grouper *Epinephelus marginatus* joins a dive.

A school of flapnose rays *Rhinoptera javanica*

ACCOMMODATION
Casa Babi is a quiet, mid-market to luxury resort right on the beach. Offers snorkelling trips and stand-up paddleboarding, and can help to organise horseriding, kitesurfing and canoeing trips.

GENERAL
Comprises: Lodge and dive centre
Website: www.odysseadive.com
Email: info@odysseadive.com
Nearest airport: Vilanculos; then 5km drive from airport
Operating since: 2002
Courses offered: PADI, DSD to DM

Denis Dujardin

A whale, like this humpback, hanging vertically in the water, is likely to be feeding its calf or cooling itself in the breeze.

The giant guitarfish *Phynchobatus dyiddensis* has the head of a ray and the body and tail of a shark.

WHEN TO GO	Sea temp	Rain	Good vis	Whales	Dolphins	Mantas	Sharks	Nudibranchs
Jan	30°C	✔			✔	✔	✔	✔
Feb	29°C	✔			✔	✔	✔	✔
Mar	28°C				✔	✔	✔	✔
Apr	26°C		✔		✔	✔	✔	✔
May	25°C		✔		✔	✔	✔	✔
Jun	24°C		✔		✔	✔	✔	✔
Jul	22°C		✔	✔	✔	✔	✔	✔
Aug	21°C		✔	✔	✔	✔	✔	✔
Sep	23°C		✔	✔	✔	✔	✔	✔
Oct	25°C		✔	✔	✔	✔	✔	✔
Nov	27°C				✔	✔	✔	✔
Dec	29°C	✔			✔	✔	✔	✔

Note: Mantas are seen only on São Sebastião. Experienced divers and excellent weather conditions are needed. Odyssea conducts dives at São Sebastião mainly in low season and rarely during the Easter holidays, in July and August or between Christmas and 7 January. There are no specifically windy months, although cyclones occur in February. Whale sharks are sometimes encountered.

WHAT THEY SAY

We offer home comfort, with small dive groups, and we speak French, Italian, Portuguese, Spanish and English.

WHAT WE SAY

Denis and Sabrina have gone out of their way to create a top-class dive resort. They have been diving the area since 2002 and their knowledge of the dives and conditions in the area is very evident.

DIVE SITE INFORMATION

The following are Odyssea's top dive sites.

Two-Mile Reef

Diver level: Any level

Highlights/Nature of dive: Two-Mile is a very wide reef that allows for varying dives depending on where one goes in and, having a max depth of 20m, easily allows for dives of 60 mins. The corals here are beautiful, very varied and in pristine condition. The reef hosts an incredible range of fish and is home to devil rays, sharpnosed stingrays and reef sharks. It is not unusual to bump into five or six massive turtles in a single dive. Between dives you can stop on Bazaruto Island to relax and enjoy amazing views of the archipelago.

Francisco Messina

Exquisite pink gorgonian fans and corals

Cabo São Sebastião

Diver level: Experienced
Highlights/Nature of dive: This is all about
wilderness, pelagics, and more. On the
surface, divers are very often welcomed by
big schools of dolphins and, from July to
October, humpback whales. The reefs are
rich in corals and reef life. You'll find mantas
being cleaned, nudibranchs, shrimps and
crabs, garden eels and schools of fusiliers.
Accessibility depends on favourable weather
and tides, which is why the reefs are still
in such pristine condition. You'll rarely
bump into another group of divers here.
The currents can be strong, so this site is
for experienced divers, diving in excellent
weather conditions only.

Francisco Messina

Juvenile star puffer *Arothron stellatus*

EXTRACTS FROM ROBYNN'S DIVE LOG

Dive #: 537	Date: 19th September		Dive Site: Two-Mile Reef
Temp: 24°C	Time: 42 mins	Depth: 27m	Rated: 4

Went out with Odyssea Dive to Bazaruto Island,
about 55 minutes away. Vis was fair (about 12m),
the water was 24°C and the site was enchantingly
beautiful. Vividly coloured fish swam over a
kaleidoscope of corals. The variety of fish was vast
and even though I saw the usual suspects for the
most part, there were just so many that I felt I had
entered fairyland.

I also saw probably the biggest turtle I've ever
encountered, sleeping in a cave.

Green turtle

Francisco Messina

Abundant reef life

Francisco Messina

Dive Bazaruto

DIVE CENTRE

🏊 On the beach

🏊 Staff assemble your dive gear (unless you prefer to do it yourself) and will rinse and hang it up after dives

DIVES

Single or double tank: As requested; if double, then there is a picnic lunch on another island during the surface interval.

Divers per group: 4–10

Leaders per group: One

Centre to launch: Directly in front of centre

Boat ride to dive sites: One hour

End of dive policy: Depends on skills and qualifications of the divers

Main attractions: Overhangs, reefs and crevices are home to a wide variety of eels – honeycomb, guineafowl and starry morays. Large schools of tuna and sierra are seen, along with big turtles, blacktip and whitetip reef sharks, mantas, devil rays, stingrays and spotted rays. There are colourful reef species such as clownfish, triggerfish, all kinds of wrasse, surgeonfish, puffers, cowfish, butterflyfish,

Moorish idols, parrotfish, scorpionfish, crocodilefish, stonefish, lionfish, pipefish and needlefish, nudibranchs and a rare frogfish. The potato bass found here weigh up to 150kg. Dolphins are often spotted from the boat, as well as whales (August–October) and, on rare occasions, even the highly endangered dugong.

BOATS

🏊 1 x 6.2m semi-rigid inflatable

🏊 1 x 9m semi-rigid inflatable

🏊 Oxygen on all boats

A common lionfish *Pterois miles* hovers midwater, displaying his splendid fins.

The beaches in the area are pristine and unspoilt.

WHEN TO GO	Sea temp	Wind/rain	Good vis	Whales	Dolphins	Mantas	Sharks	Nudibranchs
Jan	29°C	✔			✔	✔	✔	✔
Feb	29°C	✔			✔	✔	✔	✔
Mar	29°C				✔	✔	✔	✔
Apr	27°C		✔		✔	✔	✔	✔
May	25°C		✔		✔	✔	✔	✔
Jun	24°C		✔		✔	✔	✔	✔
Jul	24°C		✔		✔	✔	✔	✔
Aug	24°C	✔	✔	✔	✔	✔	✔	✔
Sep	25°C	✔	✔	✔	✔	✔	✔	✔
Oct	26°C		✔	✔	✔	✔	✔	✔
Nov	27°C				✔		✔	✔
Dec	29°C	✔			✔		✔	✔

Note: Rains occur from December to February. August and September are windy. Whale sharks are sometimes seen.

ACCOMMODATION

The dive centre is inside the Archipelago Resort, which is family-oriented in season and quiet off-season. There are self-catering Indonesian-styled casas with sea views. The resort is directly on the beach and has a restaurant. You can enjoy snorkelling or dhow trips, take part in island hopping, go whale-watching in season, or try tubing, water-skiing or deep-sea fishing.

GENERAL

Comprises: Resort with dive centre
Website: www.divebazaruto.com
Email: info@divebazaruto.com
Nearest airport: Vilanculos; then 4km by road
Operating since: 2012
Courses offered: PADI

WHAT THEY SAY

We give clients individual attention, our equipment is serviced regularly and our staff are well trained and helpful. Safety and comfort are top priorities: the owners are the instructors, ensuring top care.

WHAT WE SAY

Please note that we have not yet dived with Dive Bazaruto.

Dragon stingray *Himantura jenkinsii*

Juvenile twobar anemonefish *Amphiprion allardi*

Southern Inhambane

Southern Inhambane is known for the majesty of its
deep sea creatures. Shown here are a manta *Manta
alfredi* and a cobia *Rachycentron canadum*.

Photo: Brian Welman

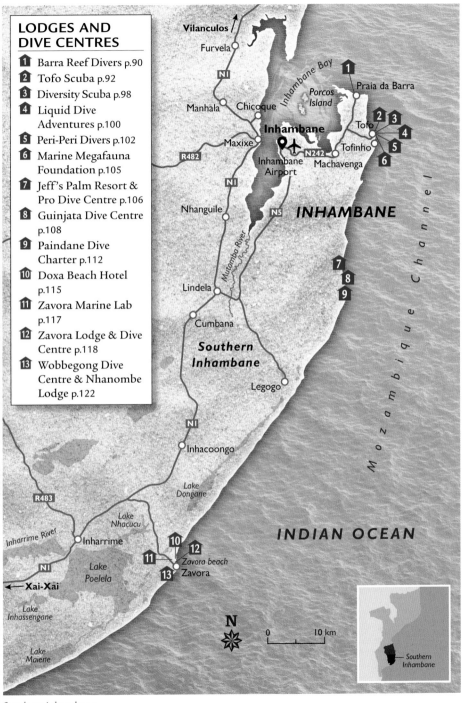

LODGES AND DIVE CENTRES

1. Barra Reef Divers p.90
2. Tofo Scuba p.92
3. Diversity Scuba p.98
4. Liquid Dive Adventures p.100
5. Peri-Peri Divers p.102
6. Marine Megafauna Foundation p.105
7. Jeff's Palm Resort & Pro Dive Centre p.106
8. Guinjata Dive Centre p.108
9. Paindane Dive Charter p.112
10. Doxa Beach Hotel p.115
11. Zavora Marine Lab p.117
12. Zavora Lodge & Dive Centre p.118
13. Wobbegong Dive Centre & Nhanombe Lodge p.122

Vilanculos
Furvela

N1

Manhala
Chicoque
Inhambane Bay
Porcos Island
Praia da Barra

1

2 3
Tofo
4
Maxixe
Inhambane
R482
N242
Tofinho
5
Inhambane Airport
Machavenga
6

N1

Nhanguile

N5 **INHAMBANE**

Mutamba River

Lindela

Cumbana

Southern Inhambane

Legogo

Porcos Island

Mozambique Channel

7
8
9

N1

Inhacoongo

Lake Dongane

R483

Lake Nhacucu

Inharrime River

Inharrime

10

12

11

Zavora beach

13
Zavora

N1

Lake Poelela

Xai-Xai

Lake Inhassengane

Lake Maiene

INDIAN OCEAN

N

0   10 km

Southern Inhambane

Southern Inhambane

Barra Reef Divers

DIVE CENTRE

- On the beach
- Adjacent to restaurants
- Dive pool

DIVES

Single or double tank: As requested
Divers per group: Usually 4–10, maximum 16
Leaders per group: Usually one, but two for training and deep dives
Centre to launch: Directly from dive centre
Boat ride to dive sites: 5–25 mins
End of dive policy: On shallow dives divers ascend when they reach 50 bar. On deep dives buddies go up in pairs when the first reaches 70 bar.
Main attractions: Mantas, humpback whales, giant morays, sharks, turtles, whale sharks, dolphins, unspoilt coral, sea horses, ghost pipefish, pansy shells, mothfish. The dive centre also offers dive charters, a dive school, snorkelling with whale sharks or sea horses, snorkelling to Pansy Island, whale-watching (humpbacks), deep-sea fishing, mangrove walks, kayaking and quad biking.

BOATS

- 3 x semi-rigid inflatables
- 1 x fibreglass fishing boat
- Oxygen on all deep-dive trips

Inside the dive centre

A whale shark *Rhincodon typus* glides peacefully past.

WHEN TO GO	Sea temp	Wind/ rain	Good vis	Whales	Whale sharks	Dolphins	Mantas	Sharks	Nudibranchs
Jan	30°C	✔	✔		✔	✔	✔	✔	✔
Feb	30°C	✔	✔		✔	✔	✔	✔	✔
Mar	29°C		✔		✔	✔	✔	✔	✔
Apr	28°C		✔		✔	✔	✔	✔	✔
May	27°C		✔			✔	✔	✔	✔
Jun	25°C			✔		✔		✔	✔
Jul	23°C			✔		✔		✔	✔
Aug	22°C			✔		✔		✔	✔
Sep	24°C			✔		✔		✔	✔
Oct	25°C	✔	✔			✔		✔	✔
Nov	27°C	✔	✔		✔	✔	✔	✔	✔
Dec	29°C	✔	✔		✔	✔	✔	✔	✔

ACCOMMODATION

You can choose between the budget, luxury or ultra-luxury resorts. All are located on the beach.

GENERAL

Comprises: Dive centre serves nearby resorts
Website: www.barrareef.co.za
Nearest airport: Inhambane; then a 25km drive
Operating since: 2002
Courses offered: PADI, CMAS, TDI and SDI

WHAT THEY SAY

If you are not a friend, we will make you one!

WHAT WE SAY

Please note that we have not yet dived with Barra Reef Divers.

Two of the semi-rigid inflatable boats

Thorny sea horse *Hippocampus histrix*

Tofo Scuba

DIVE CENTRE

🐟 Right on the beach, with hot showers and a separate customers' kit room
🐟 Impeccably maintained rental gear
🐟 Water and lollies on every dive, plus snacks on double tanks
🐟 Staff load and unload the boats
🐟 Has the only heated pool in Tofo

DIVES

Single or double tank: As requested
Divers per group: Maximum of nine
Leaders per group: Two
Centre to launch: Directly from dive centre
Boat ride to dive sites: Average 25 mins

Dive policy: Everyone stays with the group.
End of dive policy: Divers reaching 50 bar go up with one of the DMs
Main attractions: Mantas, whale sharks, potato bass, giant morays, eagle rays, whitetip reef sharks, bowmouth guitarfish, harlequin shrimps and sea moths. This is the only place in the world where you can see the smalleyed frogfish. There are also nudibranchs, dolphins, humpbacks, turtles and much more. The dive centre has a beach bar and restaurant.

BOATS

🐟 4 x 8.2m semi-rigid dive boats
🐟 Oxygen on all dive launches

Arco de Mann

Divers spending three peaceful minutes at 5m, on a safety stop

Spotted porcelain crab *Neopetrolisthes maculatus*

ACCOMMODATION

There are many places to stay nearby. Tofo Scuba is building its own accommodation, which should be ready by late 2017.

GENERAL

Comprises: Dive centre with heated pool, beach bar and restaurant
Website: www.tofoscuba.com
Email: info@tofoscuba.com
Nearest airport: Inhambane

Operating since: 1999
Courses offered: IDC centre offering courses from entry level to Instructor. PADI and IANTD.

WHEN TO GO

Mantas and whale sharks year-round. Humpbacks June–November.

Bizarre and colourful giant frogfish *Antennarius commerson*; note the feet, with which they walk instead of swimming.

Spanish dancer *Hexabranchus sanguineus*

Inhambane Province & The Bazaruto Archipelago **93**

The sun rises on another day of diving at Tofo Beach.

EXTRACTS FROM ROBYNN'S DIVE LOG

Dive #: 520	**Date:** 12th August		**Dive Site:** Manta Reef
Temp: 22°C	**Time:** 39 mins	**Depth:** 29m	**Rated:** 3

Everything at Tofo Scuba runs like a well-oiled machine. Staff friendly and helpful. Six divers and five staff on RIB. Surf entry not too hectic. About 20 minutes to get to Manta Reef. Negative entry, fair current. Plentiful fish life, including most of the usual Indian Ocean suspects – snappers, lionfish, wrasses, goldies, stonefish, huge groupers and trumpetfish come to mind. DM carrying buoyline made it easy to stay together despite poor vis. Sadly no mantas. The highlight was hearing whale song for most of the dive.

Dive #: 522	**Date:** 27th August		**Dive Site:** Giant's Castle
Temp: 22°C	**Time:** 34 mins	**Depth:** 30m	**Rated:** 4

Manta

Arco de Mann

Site is pretty much straight out from the beach, just under 5km. Negative entry as current was strong. After about 10 minutes saw first manta. So quiet and graceful. Came close to me. A bit later it came back again. Really lovely. Saw it almost head on and watched as it opened its mouth to eat. Current so strong that I was holding onto the reef with one finger so as not to get swept away. After about 20 minutes we started to head up slowly. Another manta then flew up under us. These are my first mantas ever. Both Type A* mantas. Very happy. Tofo Scuba excellently organised and good atmosphere.

WHAT THEY SAY

We pioneered diving in Tofo and found many of the reefs! We train Mozambican Divemasters and Instructors. Multiple boats mean smaller dive groups. Our operation is professionally run, never takes short cuts and has fantastic safety standards. We have four impeccable compressors and offer free Nitrox!

WHAT WE SAY

Tofo Scuba was a fun place to be – it felt like the hub of the diving action, lots going on, very knowledgeable staff, well-established routines. Having the restaurant right at the centre itself made it a natural place to hang out between dives, even on non-diving days. The smoked salmon, roasted butternut and cashew salad is a must.

DIVE SITE INFORMATION

The following are Tofo's top dive sites.

Giant's Castle

Distance to site: 8km (10 mins)
Depth: 26–33m
Bottom time: Nitrox 30 mins; air 21 mins
Highlights/Nature of dive: A 6–7m-high wall running for 2km. The wall drops from 26 to 33m and runs north/south with the predominant current. When conditions are right this is a fantastic dive, but often overlooked by divers who may know only about the more famous Manta Reef. The crenellated wall is inhabited by giant potato bass (hence the name) and features several manta-cleaning stations. Although only 10 minutes' journey from the dive centre, this is definitely a pelagic dive.

Dive #: 523	Date: 2nd September		Dive Site: Office
Temp: 22°C	Time: 28 mins	Depth: 30m	Rated: 4

This dive was truly beautiful. Negative entry, right down to about 23m and then down more slowly from there. Faffed around at the bottom waiting for someone who was struggling, but there was plenty to look at. Lots of fish, beautiful colours, despite poor vis and not much sun.

The best thing about this dive is probably the interesting topography. Lots of excellent swim-throughs, abounding with dense fish life. Beautiful nudibranchs. I found the group (about 10 of us) quite crowded and longed for my experience of diving in Oman, where we always dived in twos.

On the surface interval we slowly motored to Giant's. I lay down on the rim of the boat to try to warm up. Quite a few of the divers were seasick, but fortunately I had taken my Stugeron. Most people looked very cold, including the DMs, who were both wearing multiple suits. We saw some spectacular leaping whales very close to us, and a dolphin jumping higher out of the water than I've ever seen before.

Dive #: 524	Date: 2nd September		Dive Site: Giant's Castle
Temp: 22°C	Time: 27 mins	Depth: 27m	Rated: 3

Much less current than last time, so could relax. Saw a tiny stingray. Thought it was a baby but turns out to be a special small species seen here. On the long ascent we saw a manta swimming far below us. My third. We could hear the humpbacks calling to each other during the dive.

* Type A mantas are one of two groups of mantas, as identified by Dr Andrea Marshall of Marine Megafauna (see p.105).

EXTRACT FROM ROBYNN'S TRAVEL LOG

Day 1: Arrived in Inhambane (10th August) to find that LAM had lost my dive bag. Nobody seemed worried. Apparently this happens often and the baggage is usually found within a couple of days. Everything is wonderfully laid-back here, which is just how I remember Mozambique.

Arrived at Casa Barry, a comfortable place on the beach, with lots of reed-and-thatch bungalows of different sizes. Lovely atmosphere. Had a long walk on the beach, breakfast for supper and a good night's sleep to the sound of the sea.

Day 2: Woke up to waves lapping the shore and exquisite and unusual birdsong. In the afternoon had a good walk on the beach and went to meet the folk at Tofo Scuba. Dive planned for tomorrow. Impressively organised dive centre. Everything set up the day before.

.....

Day 6: Rain in the night. Lovely. Windy day: read, slept, did some yoga, wrote and then walked on the beach.

Day 7: The staff here at Casa Barry have invited me to have staff supper with them every night as apparently I'm now 'part of the family', according to Malcolm. Very nice of them. Lovely rain and wind.

Day 8: On the 25th I went out in the RIB on an ocean safari to look for dolphins, whales and whale sharks. During the first hour we saw only dolphins, but then suddenly spotted a whale shark. We quickly dropped into the water and looked up at the boat for direction, as you can't see once you are in the water. The skipper pointed behind me, I put my face into the water and there he was. Right there! Going past less than half a metre from me. When he swished his tail it was just centimetres from my face. I was so longing to touch him, but pulled my hand back against my body, as I knew I would be setting a poor example for those around me. I swam with him for a while until he started to go deeper and I stopped. What a special experience.

A proliferation of game fish: great barracuda, kingfish, pickhandle pike as well as various rays (manta, eagle, devil), bowmouth guitarfish, and, uniquely in Tofo, blue marlin. Divers also see a lot of hammerhead sharks on this reef.

This is an advanced drift dive with potentially strong, sometimes reverse, currents and is only suitable for advanced divers who have mastered the negative entry.

However, a descent through schools of barracuda onto a cleaning station while devil rays circle above is unforgettable. Highly recommended.

Office

Distance to site: 14km (25 mins)
Depth: 19–24m (24m max)
Bottom time: Nitrox 40 mins; air 32 mins
Highlights/Nature of dive: This is a rock pinnacle that rises from a depth of over 90m. It is primarily a drift dive, with the current running from north to south. The reef consists of a number of ledges and gullies and is an absolute must for manta enthusiasts, since mantas are seen on approximately eight out of 10 dives. On the northern point of the reef there is a station where cleaner wrasse tend to mantas. Also seen on this reef are a number of resident leopard sharks, whitetip reef sharks, potato bass, giant moray eels, turtles, tropical fish and, as the reef is 10km from shore, an abundance of game fish. This is a fairly difficult dive, because of the current, so it is recommended that you have at least 20 open-water sea dives. Vis ranges from 15 to 40m.

A passing burst of silver catches the eye.

Accommodation on the dunes at Tofo Beach

TRAVEL AND ACCOMMODATION IN TOFO

Getting there is surprisingly simple. Fly into Inhambane Airport, where someone from Tofo Scuba will meet you and take you to the hotel of your choice in the little village of Tofo, about 25 minutes away.

There are many hotels and resorts from which to choose. The ideal is to stay in the hub of things at Tofo itself, or just outside it, in Tofinho. Everything is within walking distance and all the dive centres offer transport, but if you won't have a car then it probably makes sense to be in Tofo. Book your accommodation before you go.

We can recommend Casa Barry, which offers wonderful hospitality and everything you need for a comfortable holiday. It's right in Tofo, on the beach and has its own restaurant. (Ask about the home-made cinnamon buns!) It takes 10 minutes to stroll from Casa Barry to Tofo Scuba and they cater for all budgets, except campers.

One of the things that makes Casa Barry a good place for divers is that the Whale Shark and Manta Foundation, now known as Marine Megafauna (see p.105), is based right there, with world experts Dr Andrea Marshall and Dr Simon Pearce giving fascinating slideshow talks in the evenings.

In Tofinho you'll enjoy the comparative isolation, but transport is an issue, since walking is impractical when you're carrying dive gear.

Casa Barry, one of the many places to stay at Tofo

Diversity Scuba

DIVE CENTRE

🐾 Nitrox available
🐾 Hot showers
🐾 Tea and coffee for divers

DIVES

Single or double tank: Either, depending on weather and clients' wishes
Divers per group: Between two and 10, but not more than six per diving group
Leaders per group: Two
Centre to launch: 1-min walk
Boat ride to dive sites: 10–30 mins
End of dive policy: As divers reach 50 bar they ascend with a DM; the rest continue with the other DM.
Main attractions: Sharks, mantas, macro life

BOATS

🐾 2 x Feral RIBs with 2 x Yamaha F100 4-strokes
🐾 1 x Feral RIB with 2 x Yamaha 85s
🐾 Oxygen on all boats

A skunk anemonefish *Amphiprion akallopisos* safe in its stinging home

A large potato bass *Epinephelus tukula* shows its small curved teeth, which are used to hold fish.

Leopard shark *Stegostoma fasciatum* and golden kingfish *Gnathanodon speciosus*

Yellowfin goatfish *Mulloidichthys vanicolensis* and bluebanded snappers *Lutjanus kasmira*

A manta *Manta alfredi* with attendant remoras *Echeneis naucrates*

ACCOMMODATION
This is a stand-alone dive centre, but there are several options for accommodation in the vicinity.

GENERAL
Comprises: Stand-alone dive centre
Website: www.diversityscuba.com
Email: info@diversityscuba.com
Nearest airport: Inhambane, then 21km by road
Operating since: 1999
Courses offered: All PADI courses, up to Instructor level

WHEN TO GO
Whales June–November, whale sharks and mantas all year. Water is above 25°C November–April, with best vis Jan–March. Windy in February, but changeable.

WHAT THEY SAY
Dive groups are small and we give personal service. We also offer boat trips to see whale sharks, dolphins and humpback whales.

WHAT WE SAY
We felt safe at all times with this group, as they run a tight ship and take no short cuts with safety. We were impressed that they insisted on every diver wearing a dive computer.

Liquid Dive Adventures

DIVE CENTRE
- Nitrox available
- Freediving offered
- Tea and coffee provided
- Cold showers

DIVES
Single or double tank: As requested
Divers per group: Usually six, max 12
Leaders per group: Two
Centre to launch: A 200m walk
Boat ride to dive sites: 5–30 mins
End of dive policy: Divers go up when they reach 50 bar; the rest stay down with DM
Main attractions: Lots of fish, mantas, rays, sharks, turtles, whale sharks, humpback whales. Other activities available include kayaking, snorkelling and whale-watching trips.

BOATS
- 3 x 9m rubber ducks
- Oxygen on all boats

ACCOMMODATION
Liquid offers accommodation with six rooms on the beach. They have a vegetarian restaurant..

Clown triggerfish *Balistoides conspicillum*

A view on the walk between Tofo and Tofinho

A humpback *Megaptera novaeangliae* breaches. Being underwater with one of these whales is an unforgettable experience.

GENERAL

Comprises: Dive centre with accommodation
Website: www.liquiddiveadventures.com
Email: info@liquiddiveadventures.com
Nearest airport: Inhambane, then 20km
by road
Operating since: 2005
Courses offered: PADI courses; Padi Instructor
Development Courses (IDC)

WHEN TO GO

Whales May–November; whale sharks
November–February; mantas March–June. Water
temperature above 25°C November–April

WHAT THEY SAY

Liquid Dive Adventures is a small, family-run centre where we know our divers by name. We care about conservation and give A.W.A.R.E courses about mantas, whale sharks, sharks, turtles, coral reefs and marine debris. We have a small-group policy and there are always two leaders on every dive.

WHAT WE SAY

We dived with Liquid Dive Adventures years ago, when it was under different management. We have yet to dive with them under the current ownership.

Liquid Dive Adventures

Tofo is renowned for its whale sharks *Rhincodon typus* (left) and mantas *Manta alfredi* (right).

Peri-Peri Divers

DIVE CENTRE

🐟 Nitrox available
🐟 Showers available
🐟 Free tea and coffee

DIVES

Single or double tank: As requested
Divers per group: 5–8
Leaders per group: Always two
Centre to launch: Five mins down steps and along the beach; surf entries, as with all diving in Tofo
Boat ride to dive sites: 10–40 mins
End of dive policy: Divers low on air go up with one DM while the others finish out their bottom time.
Main attractions: Mantas, whale sharks, humpback whales as well as great macro diving.

Owner Nick writes, 'My best dive day ever was in August one year. We went to Giant's Castle and had a 4m great white circling. Went back to Giant's the same day and had eight humpback whales swim past with 20m vis. I still get excited talking about it.'

A shoal of snappers *Lutjanus* spp. bursts apart in front of a diver.

A whitetip reef shark *Triaenodon obesus* allows some fascinated divers to get close.

A diver assesses a swim-through.

Final checks in the last minutes before a dive

BOATS

🐾 2 x semi-rigid inflatable ducks, with 4-stroke Suzuki motors, one with 90h.p., the other with 115h.p.

🐾 Water and lollipops provided on boats for single dives

🐾 Bananas, biscuits, tea and coffee provided for double dives

🐾 Oxygen on all trips

ACCOMMODATION

Quiet, family resort. Simple and beachy, on top of a hill, one minute from the sea.

GENERAL

Comprises: Independent dive centre with its own resort
Website: www.peri-peridivers.com
Email: nick@peri-peridivers.com
Nearest airport: Inhambane, then 30 mins by road
Operating since: 2009
Courses offered: All PADI courses up to Assistant Instructor (AI)

WHEN TO GO

Whales July–October, whale sharks November–June, reef mantas year-round, but giant mantas March–May. North wind brings lots of plankton so there are sharks. South wind brings great vis.

Frida Milice

Delicately beautiful soft corals

WHAT THEY SAY

We are a fun, owner-operated centre, offering a highly personalised service. Nick and Steve (owners) actively participate in most dives. We love what we do and it shows.

WHAT WE SAY

A professionally run dive centre where all your needs are taken care of and you immediately feel at home. The people are warmly welcoming – you'll definitely want to go back.

A diver encounters a honeycomb moray *Gymnothorax favagineus*.

Sea goldies *Pseudanthias squamipinnis* and a tailspot squirrelfish *Sargocentron caudimaculatum* swim around a colourful bommie.

Marine Megafauna Foundation

One of the most interesting places we have visited in Mozambique is the Marine Megafauna Foundation (MMF), based at the Tree House on Tofo Beach. It is a non-profit organisation created in 2009 to research, protect and conserve marine megafauna – that is, populations of large species such as sharks, rays, marine mammals and turtles – worldwide.

According to the MMF, these animals are key components of marine ecosystems but, as they

Dr Andrea Marshall hovering near a large reef manta.

are long-lived and have low reproductive rates, they are usually the first to suffer population declines because of human pressure. Fortunately, they are also among the most charismatic animals on the planet and engender a high degree of public interest in their biology and conservation, making them useful ambassadors for the whole marine environment.

MMF's research in Mozambique focuses on manta rays, *Manta alfredi* and *Manta birostris*, and whale sharks *Rhincodon*. These huge plankton-feeders congregate along the southern coast of Mozambique. The organisation also examines other species threatened in Mozambique, such as sea turtles, dugongs and the small-eyed stingray. For more information about their work, visit **www.marinemegafauna.org**.

 MARINE MEGAFAUNA FOUNDATION

The whale shark *Rhincodon typus* is a gentle giant.

Jeff's Palm Resort & Pro Dive Centre

DIVE CENTRE

- PADI five-star dive centre on the beach
- Nitrox available
- Hot showers with private changing rooms

Crescent-tail bigeyes *Priacanthus hamrur*

DIVES

Single or double tank: Usually return between dives, but will do double tanks if requested

Divers per group: Maximum of 12

Leaders per group: One DM per six divers

Centre to launch: Directly from centre

Boat ride to dive sites: 5–25 mins

End of dive policy: Will attempt to match divers with similar air consumption

Main attractions: The world-famous Manta Reef with its permanent manta-cleaning station, whale sharks, dolphins, humpback whales (in season), nudibranchs, sea moths, gurnets, paperfish, longnose hawkfish, porcelain crabs, crocodile flatheads and a huge variety of macro and pelagic life.

A potato bass *Epinephelus tukula* amid a shoal of slender sweepers *Parapriacanthus ransonneti*

The sun rises over the sea at Jeff's Palm Resort.

BOATS

🐟 2 x 8.5m semi-rigid inflatables (rubber ducks)
🐟 Oxygen on all boats

ACCOMMODATION

Peaceful, beachy, beautiful, self-catering, family-oriented, perfect for parties of divers. There are comfortable reed-and-thatch casas and cabanas on the dunes overlooking the sea. Each casa or cabana can sleep beween six and 10 people and many offer en-suite bathrooms.

GENERAL

Comprises: Resort and dive centre
Website: jeffsprodive.com
Email: diving@jeffsmoz.com
Phone: +258 842 39 1100
Nearest airport: Inhambane; then 30km by road
Operating since: Resort 2003, dive centre 2006
Courses offered: All PADI courses

WHEN TO GO

Diving is good all year. Humpbacks from end of June to October. Whale sharks year-round, but best August–April. Mantas all year. Water 21°C in winter, 29°C in summer. Best vis March and April. Windy in February.

WHAT THEY SAY

We offer excellent customer service combined with serious fun and a relaxing atmosphere. The resort, restaurant and dive centre are right on the beach and provide everything a diver needs for a superb holiday.

WHAT WE SAY

A great place with superb diving, the centre is efficiently run by people who know the sites well and care about giving divers the best possible experience.

Beautiful harlequin shrimp *Hymenocera picta* at Pao Reef

Guinjata Dive Centre

DIVE CENTRE

🐾 Right on the beach
🐾 Showers and toilets
🐾 Braai facilities and pizza nights on the beach
🐾 Staff will rinse and hang up your gear after dives

DIVES

Single or double tank: As requested
Divers per group: Maximum of 10
Leaders per group: One
Centre to launch: Launch directly from the dive centre
Boat ride to dive sites: 3–15 mins
End of dive policy: Group stays together; each buddy pair ascends when one of them reaches 50 bar.

Main attractions: Pristine reefs, including the world-famous Manta Reef with its cleaning station and year-round mantas. Many sites are ideal for night diving. They offer courses in diving (see 'Courses offered') and underwater photography. The 'Love the Ocean' volunteer programme is run at various times throughout the year.

Guests attend a PADI rescue course

Bommies brim with life; here a diver fins past, enjoying the spectacle.

This lucky diver is having a close encounter with a whale shark *Rhincodon typus*.

BOATS

🐾 2 x Superducks with 4-stroke engines
🐾 Oxygen on all boats

ACCOMMODATION

They have their own divers' house, and will also help guests find accommodation – from campsites to self-catering options to private houses.

GENERAL

Comprises: Stand-alone dive centre
Website: www.diveguinjata.com
Email: lynn@diveguinjata.com
Phone: +258 84 401 5449
Nearest airport: Inhambane
Operating since: 2003
Courses offered: PADI, IANTD, SSI and HSA

A group heads out from the dive centre on one of the rubber ducks.

WHEN TO GO

Diving is good all year. April–September slightly cooler. Humpbacks June–November. Whale sharks and mantas throughout the year, but far more common in summer.

Jack Mifflin

A rare sighting of a sea moth *Eurypegasus draconis*

WHAT THEY SAY

People keep coming back to Guinjata because we have a great team and we all enjoy diving every day. We have five instructors, one DM and five skippers. You can do all your training here and we also run courses for free divers and the disabled.

WHAT WE SAY

The beauty of diving here is that most of the dive sites (including the world-famous Manta Reef) are right on your doorstep. Many sites are just moments away – you can reach the furthest sites within 12 minutes. There is a restaurant on the beach, right next door to the dive centre. The staff are very helpful, friendly, relaxed and professional.

EXTRACTS FROM ROBYNN'S DIVE LOG

Dive #: 529	Date: 9th September		Dive Site: Manta Reef
Temp: 20°C	Time: 44 mins	Depth: 24m	Rated: 4

Went out with Guinjata Divers. Only four of us, which was lovely. Approached from a different side to the last time I dived here, so boat trip much shorter (about 12 minutes). No mantas, but a sudden flock of about 10 devil rays flew past in formation.

Dive #: 530	Date: 10th September		Dive Site: Pao
Temp: 23°C	Time: 54 mins	Depth: 18m	Rated: 4

Went out with Guinjata Divers again. Saw three gorgeous big cowries together in a cave. Also a paperfish, lots of lionfish, including a tiny 5cm baby in a plant. Three juvenile emperor angelfish, exquisite bright yellow trumpetfish, and some mantis shrimps. Baby bluespotted stingray, fascinating sea snake (or possibly a snake eel; it was too active for me to be sure.) Dive is directly off the beach from which Guinjata launches, and takes about 4 minutes to reach. Very little effort for a beautiful dive.

Dive #: 532	Date: 13th September		Dive Site: Manta Reef
Temp: 23°C	46 mins	Depth: 27m	Rated: 4

My third visit to this reef. Went out with Guinjata again. Fantastic vis – about 25m. But alas, still haven't seen any mantas.

Saw my first dragon eel. Did a 'dance' with a potato bass, and the DM got it on film. Then on the way back we saw a mother and baby humpback close by, and got into the water. They left quite quickly, but I still got to see them underwater. Very special moment.

The round ribbontail ray *Taeniura meyeni* inhabits sandy areas.

EXTRACTS FROM ROSS'S DIVE LOG

Location: Manta Reef – Guinjata Dive Centre   **Date:** 4th July
Vis: 15m   **Dive time:** 48 mins   **Water temp:** 20°C   **Max depth:** 29m (avg 22m)
Comments: Calm sea, 2m swells with some surge; pleasure dive

Great dive. Twenty-minute boat ride to Manta Reef.
Quiet descent to pinnacles at north end. Lots of fish of
all types (angelfish, idols, parrotfish, goldies, etc). Also
stonefish and lionfish in a cave. Big potato bass hiding
in cave. Many anemones and big spiny sea urchins
30cm across. Nine manta rays as close as 1m. Hid
behind reef as mantas swam/flew through cleaning
station high above us. Stunning and huge – 3m across!
On ascent saw three devil rays swimming past in mid-water. Bottlenose dolphins
on return trip. According to DM, rays average 4–6m with maximum 9m.

Diver and manta

Zelda Norden

Location: Green Tree Deep Ledge – Guinjata Dive Centre   **Date:** 5th July
Vis: 15m   **Dive time:** 38 mins   **Water temp:** 24°C   **Max depth:** 33m
Comments: Sea choppy/rough; pleasure/deep dive

Rough sea made for a bumpy ride. Descended to reef at 30m and moved over to ledge. Many big
green tree corals, amazing due to their rareness in the region. Goldies, damsels and other small fish
flitting around the branches. Big game fish (kingfish, grouper and yellowtail) seaward of ledge. Swam
south to 32m with lionfish visible under ledges and little caves. One coral had a 1.5m honeycomb
moray draped over it. On boat ride back we snorkelled briefly with an 8m whale shark – wow!

Paindane
Dive Charter

DIVE CENTRE

- Nitrox available
- Hot showers
- Cold orange juice
- They offer snorkelling and trips to see whales, whale sharks and dolphins

DIVES

Single or double tank: Double on request, but generally return to the centre between dives
Divers per group: Usually about 15 in season and 10 out of season
Leaders per group: One DM per eight divers
Centre to launch: 600m
Boat ride to dive sites: 5–35 mins
End of dive policy: Buddy pairs ascend when first diver reaches 50 bar or 50 mins

Main attractions: Pristine reefs and an abundance of varied marine species, from the tiniest nudibranchs to leatherback and loggerhead turtles to mantas, whales and whale sharks.

BOATS

- 2 x 8.2m RIBs
- Oxygen sets on all boats
- Water and lollies after the dive

ACCOMMODATION

There are many resorts in the area, all of which dive with Paindane Dive Charter. We stayed at Paindane Beach Resort, which is rustic, beachy, peaceful and family-oriented, with basic but comfortable chalets overlooking the sea.

Reef scene with yellow-lined fusiliers *Caesio varilineata*

Nudibranch *Siboga cuthona*

GENERAL

Comprises: Paindane Dive Charter and Water Sport Centre, catering for multiple resorts

Website: www.divepaindane.com and www.paindanelodge.co.za

Email: vossie.divepaindane@gmail.com

Nearest airport: Inhambane

Operating since: 2006

Courses offered: CMAS and IANTD, SDI/TDI, SSI, Open Water, Trimix, Nitrox, Cave Diver and other specialties

PAINDANE BEACH RESORT

Paindane Beach Resort is basic but comfortable. Houses of varying sizes are nicely situated on dunes above the sea. This might be the place to come if you're a large group looking for simple accommodation in a beautiful setting. The house where we stayed had seven single beds and a double. Its best feature was the large verandah facing the sea; the second best was that you could watch the whales while you showered!

The houses each have a basic kitchen, so you can take the self-catering route if you wish – always useful for divers with their odd schedules. There is a small shop next to reception for basics such as milk, bread and toiletries.

A happy find is the resort's Wellness Centre, just above the beach, which offers massages for tired bodies and is also a way to keep non-diving partners happy.

The walk from the houses to the dive centre is quite demanding and in deep sand, but Vossie Vosloo, who runs the dive centre, kindly offered us lifts in his interesting vehicle.

EXTRACTS FROM ROBYNN'S DIVE LOG

Dive #: 531	Date: 11th September		Dive Site: Paindane Reef
Temp: 23°C	Time: 42 mins	Depth: 28m	Rated: 4

Vossie Vosloo took me on a special guided tour of this famous reef, about 800m from the shore, directly out from Paindane Beach Resort (and my cottage, number 10.) What a beautiful reef. Even better than Pao, and it stretches on and on. Big game fish above and coral fish near the bottom. Just lovely everywhere. Saw all the usual Indian Ocean suspects, but lots of them at a time. Loud whale song throughout the dive. For most of the dive we drifted gently with the current. One fabulous moment when we soared over the edge of a wall and dropped down the other side. Like flying. Heaven.

WHEN TO GO

Whales late May to November; whale sharks October–May; mantas most of the year. Water temperature 27°C in summer, 22°C in winter. Best vis March–July. Intermittent rain and wind October–February.

WHAT THEY SAY

We try to provide friendly, safe and individual service. We know the reef and its creatures intimately and provide excellent technical service to our divers. Our motto is 'Our best is the least we can do'.

WHAT WE SAY

The dive centre, which is well equipped and right on the beach, is run by Vossie Vosloo, a local legend who has been diving these reefs for many years. Vossie knows the reefs here very well and it's clear that he runs the centre in a safe and professional manner.

Nudibranch *Hypselodoris regina*

A large manta ray *Manta alfredi* surrounded by various brightly coloured species on a sunny day

Doxa Beach Hotel

DIVE CENTRE

🐾 Nitrox offered
🐾 Tea and coffee for divers

DIVES

Single or double tank: Usually double
Divers per group: 2–6
Leaders per group: Two
Centre to launch: 1km
Boat ride to dive sites: 15–25 mins
End of dive policy: Divers reaching 50 bar
go up with a DM
Main attractions: Mantas, sea turtles, giant
groupers, whales, many nudibranch species,
wrecks and, sometimes, whale sharks
and dolphins

BOATS

🐾 1 x semi-rigid duck
🐾 Water and fruit on boats
🐾 Oxygen on all boats

Doxa's Lodge

A snorkeller enjoying the experience of a lifetime with a whale shark *Rhincodon typus*

ACCOMMODATION

Quiet, peaceful, family-oriented luxury resort. Situated on a dune on the beach. Diving, horseriding, snorkelling. Huge deck area with swimming pool. Fantastic for whale-watching season.

GENERAL

Comprises: Resort with its own dive centre; Doxa uses its own dive centre or sends its divers to dive with Zavora Lodge Dive Centre, depending on various factors.
Website: www.doxabeachhotel.co.za
Email: doxabeach@yahoo.co.za
Nearest airport: Inhambane; then 90km south by road
Operating since: 2015
Courses offered: PADI, IANTD; courses currently offered through Zavora Lodge

WHEN TO GO

November–March good vis, water 28°C and a good chance of seeing mantas. June–October water below 26°C; whales and mantas present. Rainy November–February; windy in August.

WHAT THEY SAY

Our resort is newly built and top quality. We offer luxury accommodation with fine dining. Our deck and swimming pool area is perfect for whale-watching and cooling off. We are in the remote region of Zavora, which means that you can relax, swim, dive, snorkel or ride horses on the beach in a quiet and unspoilt environment.

WHAT WE SAY

We have not yet dived with Doxa Beach Hotel.

Nudibranch *Nembrotha purpureolineata*

Riding on unspoilt beaches is a memorable experience.

Zavora Marine Lab

Divers interested in marine research and conservation might like to visit the Zavora Marine Lab, which takes advantage of the pristine nature of the remote Zavora reefs to do scientific diving. Their research focuses on manta rays, nudibranchs, sea horses, humpback whales and wreck colonisation.

According to Zavora Marine Lab, mantas occur year-round at Zavora (peaking June–September). The lab is conducting photo-identification research, and the resulting data is being used to assist in the conservation of Zavora's manta populations.

They are also the first lab to be conducting research on Mozambique's nudibranchs – these beautifully vibrant sea slugs are among the most diverse groups of marine invertebrate. So far, more than 270 species have been found in Zavora, 90% of which are being recorded here for the first time, and 30 of which are completely new to science.

Zavora Lab also created a monitoring programme to evaluate reef colonisation on a wreck that sunk in 2013. Benthic and fish surveys are done using substrate photos, video transects and stationary fish census. This offers a unique opportunity for divers to do some wreck diving while helping to evaluate ecosystem health.

During humpback season (July–November) land-based surveys also take place. Using tail fluke photo-identification, assessments are performed to estimate the relative population structure of humpback whales in Zavora Bay. Zavora is said to be the humpback capital of Mozambique and whether you are participating in land-based surveys or listening to whale songs underwater, you will understand why!

Nudibranch *Hypselodoris pulchella*

In addition to all the amazing species in these research projects, many other coral, invertebrate, fish, turtle, and shark species can be seen in Zavora Bay.

The lab offers internships to those interested in helping with their research, as well as an opportunity for students to carry out their own projects. See more at **www.marineactionresearch.com**.

Nudibranch *Cratena affinis*

Zavora Lodge & Dive Centre

DIVE CENTRE
- Nitrox available
- Towels provided
- Tea and coffee provided

DIVES
Single or double tank: As requested
Divers per group: 12
Leaders per group: Two
Centre to launch: 1km

Boat ride to dive sites: 2–11km
End of dive policy: We end the dive on 50 bar or 60 mins
Main attractions: Wrecks, mantas, whales. Also offer ocean safaris, night dives and snorkelling.

BOATS
- Two rubber ducks
- Water on boats
- Oxygen on all dive trips

Divers explore the propeller of the *Klipfontein*, a Dutch liner that sank in 1953 after hitting a foreign object.

A diver captures a treasured moment with a manta *Manta alfredi*

ACCOMMODATION

A simple family resort that is right on the beach.

GENERAL

Comprises: Resort with its own dive centre
Website: www.zavoralodge.com
Email: reservations@zavoralodge.com
Province: Inhambane
Nearest airport: Inhambane; then 110km by road
Operating since: 2007
Courses offered: NAUI (National Association of Underwater Instructors) and DAN

A young child captivated and totally relaxed underwater

Gem nudibranch *Goniobranchus geminus*

Pincushion starfish *Culcita schmideliana*

WHEN TO GO	Sea temp	Wind/ rain	Good vis	Whales	Whale sharks	Dolphins	Mantas	Sharks	Nudibranchs
Jan	26+°C	✔	✔		✔	✔		✔	✔
Feb	26+°C	✔	✔		✔	✔		✔	✔
Mar	26°C	✔	✔			✔		✔	✔
Apr	26°C	✔	✔			✔		✔	✔
May	24°C		✔			✔	✔	✔	✔
Jun	23°C		✔	✔		✔	✔	✔	✔
Jul	22°C	✔		✔		✔	✔	✔	✔
Aug	21°C	✔		✔		✔	✔	✔	✔
Sep	21°C	✔	✔	✔		✔	✔	✔	✔
Oct	24°C		✔		✔	✔	✔	✔	✔
Nov	26°C	✔	✔		✔	✔	✔	✔	✔
Dec	26°C	✔	✔		✔	✔		✔	✔

Note: It may be rainy from November to April. July to September are windy.

WHAT THEY SAY

We offer nitrox, wreck dives, technical dives, mantas, deep dives and shallow dives. We have abundant life on our reefs.

WHAT WE SAY

The diving here was fabulous. For details of what makes Zavora so special, see the dive log on the opposite page.

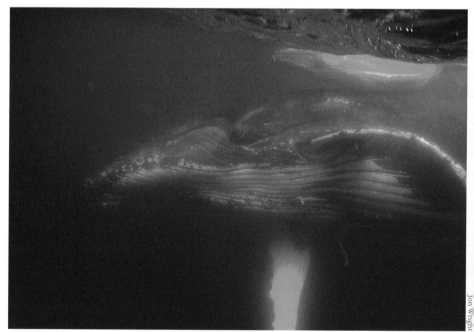

Jon Wright

Getting this close to a humpback whale *Megaptera novaeangliae* underwater is never forgotten.

| **Dive #:** 525 | **Date:** 5th September | | **Dive Site:** Deep Reef South |
| **Temp:** 21°C | **Time:** 54 mins | **Depth:** 32m | **Rated:** 4 |

This is a beautiful site, teeming with fish, lots of colour, lots of current, interesting topography. Exquisite colours and a great swim-through. On the way there we had a special moment. A large female humpback had her tail flukes high, high in the air. The power of her muscles was amazing. She just hung there, seeming quite comfortable, while her baby swam around her at the surface. At one stage the baby swam about halfway to our boat and then went back to her mom. We switched off the engines and sat, completely silent, watching in awe as the mother just hung there, her huge, muscular black tail gleaming in the sun, about 15m away. Spellbinding.

| **Dive #:** 527 | **Date:** 6th September | | **Dive Site:** Arcadia |
| **Temp:** 23°C | **Time:** 42 mins | **Depth:** 32m | **Rated:** 5 |

Today on the way out, we saw the mother and baby humpbacks again, playing together at the surface. The size of the mother's back as it arched out of the water was breathtaking. The baby seemed to be practising jumping out of the water, as it did so over and over again, coming closer and closer to us. We just sat dead still, with the engines off in the middle of the ocean. Suddenly the whales turned towards us and the mother dived right next to us – in our little RIB boat – and then dived under us! The baby followed. The water churned on both sides of us; it was wonderful.

Absolutely beautiful dive. Again, the topography is very interesting, with one particularly lovely swim-through (which I did alone), leading to a wonderland of colours and fish and beauty.

There suddenly appeared a very big grouper – about 1.5m. It seemed to want to play with one of the guys, but he curled up his knees under his chin for protection. Then the grouper chose me and I was just fascinated to be so close to such an amazing animal; he was centimetres from my face, staring right into my eyes. So I started to 'dance' with him, and he swam with me and turned with me, always looking deep into my eyes and remaining close to my face. What an amazing experience. Strong current, lovely dive.

| **Dive #:** 528 | **Date:** 6th September | | **Dive Site:** White Sands |
| **Temp:** 20°C | **Time:** 40 mins | **Depth:** 11m | **Rated:** 3 |

Looked like pea soup going in, but as we swam north it cleared fairly nicely. Saw my first Spanish dancer. I was surprised by the size of it – much bigger than most other nudibranchs. Then saw two more later. Again, fascinating topography; it felt as if we were the first explorers – and we just about were. A very newly discovered site. Each time divers drop in they go different ways, as the site is very expansive. I was cold, but it was worth staying for the exhilarating sense of exploration.

Dennis King

Green tree coral

Wobbegong Dive Centre & Nhanombe Lodge

DIVE CENTRE

- Hot showers, tea, coffee
- Nitrox available
- Water and lollipops on single tanks
- Water, refreshments, lollipops and optional boat pack on double tanks

DIVES

Single or double tank: As requested

Divers per group: Maximum of seven in a group and 14 on a boat

Leaders per group: One or two, depending on the number of divers

The striking colours and markings of the common lionfish *Pterois miles* indicate its toxicity.

The broadclub cuttlefish *Sepis latimanus* is a fascinating, communicative creature.

Centre to launch: By car or foot
Boat ride to dive sites: 15–30 mins
End of dive policy: Depending on the conditions and divers' experience they may call the dive when the first person reaches 70 bar or allow two divers who are low on air to ascend as a buddy team along the buoy line carried by the dive leader.
Main attractions: In season mantas, whale sharks, humpbacks, over 300 species of nudibranch, crocodilefish, leopard sharks, hammerheads, bullsharks, frogfish, whitetip reef sharks and large stingrays. There are also wrecks for tech divers and much more.

Humpback whales enter the bay in late June and leave in October. Peak season is July to September. Although whale shark sightings have been rare lately, tagging research shows they are still coming to Zavora. This is nudibranch paradise: over 250 species that are known of and likely many more to be discovered! They are found year-round.

BOATS

🐾 1 x 8m Superduck
🐾 Oxygen on all trips

©www.smishyfish.co.za 2017

Zebra moray *Gymnomuraena zebra*

A brilliantly camouflaged scorpionfish *Scorpaenopsis* sp.

WHEN TO GO	Sea temp	Wind/rain	Good vis	Whales	Mantas	Nudibranchs
Jan	26°C	✔	✔		✔	✔
Feb	29°C	✔	✔		✔	✔
Mar	28°C	✔	✔		✔	✔
Apr	28°C		✔		✔	✔
May	26°C		✔		✔	✔
Jun	24°C		✔	✔	✔	✔
Jul	23°C			✔	✔	✔
Aug	23°C	✔		✔	✔	✔
Sep	24°C		✔	✔	✔	✔
Oct	25°C		✔	✔	✔	✔
Nov	26°C	✔	✔		✔	✔
Dec	27°C	✔	✔		✔	✔

Note: Peak season for whales runs from July to September. There's a slight chance of rain between November and February; it is windy in August, and sometimes also in February and March.

ACCOMMODATION

Wobbegong divers stay at Nhanombe Lodge in a bush camp setting behind the beach dune. It is peaceful and quiet, suiting everyone, including families. Party people enjoy the bar. Campsites are available with hot showers and an electrical point. They also offer snorkelling, ocean safaris, a small library and horseriding.

GENERAL

Comprises: Resort and dive centre
Website: www.wobbegongdive.co.za and www.nhanombelodge.com
Email: info@wobbegongdive.co.za and info@nhanombelodge.com
Nearest airport: Inhambane; then 80km by road
Operating since: 2014
Courses offered: PADI five-star IDC centre, so all courses

WHAT THEY SAY

Service is our top priority. We do everything possible to make our guests happy. All of our staff are passionate about diving and excited to show our guests the beautiful dive sites around Zavora. Our chef will be your host for meals and take care of your personal requests for breakfasts after your first dive. We have the best pizza in the area, made in our own wood-fired pizza oven. Join our pizza evenings for a whole lot of fun. We are dedicated to making your stay and dives with us something to remember. Join our family!

WHAT WE SAY

We have not yet dived with Wobbegong or stayed at Nhanombe.

Supplied by Wobbegong Dive

Nudibranch *Nembrotha purpureolineata*

Maputo Province

Night diving is always an unforgettable experience.
Photo: Peter Pinnock

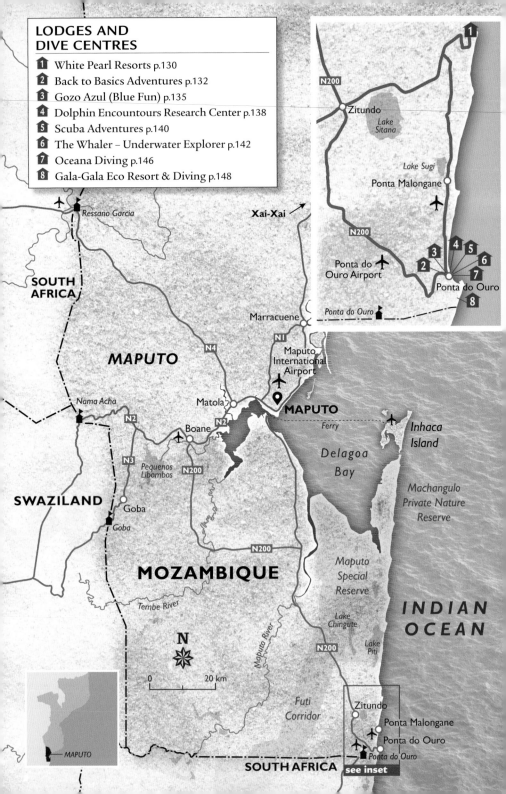

LODGES AND DIVE CENTRES

1. White Pearl Resorts p.130
2. Back to Basics Adventures p.132
3. Gozo Azul (Blue Fun) p.135
4. Dolphin Encountours Research Center p.138
5. Scuba Adventures p.140
6. The Whaler – Underwater Explorer p.142
7. Oceana Diving p.146
8. Gala-Gala Eco Resort & Diving p.148

Ressano Garcia

Xai-Xai

N200

Zitundo

Lake Sitana

Lake Sugi

Ponta Malongane

Ponta do Ouro Airport

N200

SOUTH AFRICA

Marracuene

N1

Maputo International Airport

N4

Ponta do Ouro

Ponta do Ouro

Nama Acha

Matola

MAPUTO

N2

Boane

N2

Ferry

Inhaca Island

Delagoa Bay

N3

Pequenos Libombos

N200

SWAZILAND

Goba

Goba

Machangulo Private Nature Reserve

MOZAMBIQUE

Tembe River

N200

Maputo Special Reserve

Lake Chingute

INDIAN OCEAN

N

Maputo River

0   20 km

Lake Piti

N200

Futi Corridor

Zitundo

Ponta Malongane

Ponta do Ouro

MAPUTO

Ponta do Ouro

SOUTH AFRICA   see inset

M aputo is the most southerly of Mozambique's provinces and shares a border with South Africa. This fact is central to the diving industry of the area, as it is reasonably easy for South Africans driving from Durban or Johannesburg to reach the diving zone, known as 'The Pontas', in just a few hours.

The word *Ponta* means 'point', or 'tip', and is used to describe geographical points jutting out to form a bay. Virtually all the diving in the south of Mozambique takes place around the small village of Ponta do Ouro and the nearby Ponta Mamoli and Ponta Malongane.

Most of the resorts in this area cater for families and groups of divers coming across from South Africa and are among the most affordable in Mozambique. They range from simple campsites to comfortable lodges.

During South African school holidays Ponta thrums with life. Resorts and boats are full and there is a vibrant atmosphere. If you prefer your dive holiday quieter, then make sure you go outside of these times. Summers are hot, and it is mild in winter. The 25 or so dive sites offer a wide range of experiences, from easy, shallow dives of indescribable colour (Doodles) to one of the top shark dives in the world (Pinnacles). You won't be disappointed if you choose your timing carefully. We saw both bullsharks and hammerhead sharks. Humpback whales can also be seen in season, between July and November, peaking in August and September. Check the timing grids on the resort pages.

Please note that, because Ponta's dive centres and dive sites are so close to each other, this chart applies to all of them.

Hilary Jenkins

Scalloped hammerhead *Sphyrna lewini*

WHEN TO VISIT	Sea temp	Wind/ rain	Good vis	Whales	Sharks	Dolphins	Mantas	Nudibranchs
Jan	27°C		✔		✔	✔		✔
Feb	27°C		✔		✔	✔		✔
Mar	27°C		✔		✔	✔		✔
Apr	26°C		✔		✔	✔		✔
May	24°C		✔		✔	✔	✔	✔
Jun	23°C		✔		✔		✔	✔
Jul	22°C		✔	✔	✔			✔
Aug	18°C	✔	✔	✔	✔	✔		
Sep	19°C	✔	✔	✔	✔	✔		
Oct	22°C	✔	✔	✔	✔	✔		✔
Nov	24°C		✔		✔	✔		✔
Dec	26°C		✔		✔	✔		✔

Note: Whale sharks are very rarely seen. Vis is about 15m year-round. Peak time for sharks is from November–February. Mantas are encountered about 5 per cent of the time during the months of May and June, but are otherwise not encountered.

White Pearl Resorts

DIVE CENTRE

🐾 This dive centre, at Ponta Mamoli, is right on the beach

🐾 Boats launch directly from the centre

🐾 Hot showers are available

🐾 Water is provided on all boats

DIVES

Single or double tank: Usually return between dives but will do double tanks on request

Divers per group: Max of eight

DMs per group: Two

Launch: Directly from the centre

Boat ride to dive sites: About 10 mins

Dive policy: Buddy pairs must stay together.

End of dive policy: One DM comes up with early ascenders, the other stays down for those with more air.

BOATS

🐾 1 x rubber duck with 2 x 4-stroke 100h.p. Yamaha engines

🐾 Oxygen on all boats

Sea slug *Chelidonura punctata*

Pods of friendly dolphins, like these pantropical spotted dolphins *Stenella attenuata*, can often be seen in the shallows here.

Aerial view of White Pearl Resorts

ACCOMMODATION

Peaceful, luxurious family and honeymoon resort. Activities include swimming in the pool, ocean safaris, horseriding, town tours, beach picnics, spa treatments, turtle walks, beach sports and stargazing.

GENERAL

Comprises: Resort and dive centre
Website: www.whitepearlresorts.com
Email: activities@whitepearlresorts.com
Nearest airport: Maputo
Operating since: 2002
Courses offered: PADI; children aged eight and over can also be introduced to diving by means of a Bubblemaker course.

WHAT THEY SAY

We offer a safe, professional, world-class diving experience with multitudes of fish, vibrant corals and exhilarating shark sightings on one of the world's top pinnacle reefs. We launch directly from the resort. Two species of turtle nest along our beaches. PADI courses are available for all. Whale season lasts from July to November and affords a unique opportunity to encounter these majestic animals. With a myriad sea creatures and beautiful reefs, this is the perfect underwater canvas for diving photography.

WHAT WE SAY

We have yet to dive with this resort.

Ocean and pool: the best of both worlds on your doorstep

Back to Basics Adventures

DIVE CENTRE

🐟 Good rental equipment
🐟 Hot and cold showers, toilet
🐟 Free tea and coffee
🐟 Reference books
🐟 Comfortable relaxing area
🐟 100m from beach
🐟 Staff help prepare for dive and rinse all gear afterwards

DIVES

Single or double tank: Usually single, returning between dives
Divers per group: Average of four
DMs per group: One
Centre to launch: About 8 mins (1km), on a trailer with seats
Boat ride to dive sites: 5–35 mins

Dive policy: DM must be able to see all divers at all times
End of dive policy: Divers with long air usage can stay down until DM gets to 50 bar, or 5 mins before deco

Soft coral goby *Pleurosicya boldinghi*

Close encounter with a Zambezi shark (bullshark) *Carcharhinus leucas*

Wild Indian Ocean bottlenose dolphins *Tursiops aduncus* sometimes approach and interact with snorkellers.

Main attractions: Pelagics, sharks and nudibranchs; nitrox is available if pre-arranged three weeks in advance.

BOATS

🐾 I x rubber duck
🐾 Oxygen on boat for every dive
🐾 Water and towels supplied on boat

ACCOMMODATION

For basic accommodation you can arrange with the dive centre to hire the house across the road. Alternatively you can book into one of the many resorts nearby. The owners of the dive centre will help you to choose one if you ask.

GENERAL

Comprises: Dive centre and accommodation
Website: www.backtobasicsadventures.com
Email: jstromvoll@gmail.com
Nearest airport: Maputo
Courses offered: PADI

Other activities offered: Quadbike rental, ocean safaris, snorkelling trips, Kosi Bay trips, safaris at Tembe Elephant Park.

WHAT THEY SAY

We are a boutique dive charter where each diver is known by name. We offer shallow and deep dives according to your qualifications. There is no adventure within your comfort zone!

A humpback whale *Megaptera novaeangliae* swims right up to the boat.

Nudibranch *Favorinus tsuruganus*

WHAT WE SAY

Jenny Stromvoll and Rupert Cornelius run an excellent dive centre. From the moment you arrive here you know that every need will be taken care of with expertise and a smile. The centre is at their house, shaded by big trees, with every facility you could ask for. The staff are helpful and well trained. Once people have dived with Jenny and Rupert, they tend to keep coming back. Groups wanting to specialise in shark or nudibranch dives have experts on hand. Highly recommended.

EXTRACTS FROM ROBYNN'S DIVE LOG

Dive #: 771	Date: 23rd February		Dive Site: Atlantis
Temp: 26°C	Time: 38 mins	Depth: 43.5m	Rated: 3

Yet another beautiful dive with Back to Basics. The sea is almost unbelievably blue. Twelve of us on the boat. Clear at the bottom, 11 minutes of beauty, then suddenly it was as if someone had dumped a vat of milk into the sea — so very cloudy that you could only see about 2m around you. We didn't see anything after that.

Dive #: 772	Date: 24th February		Dive Site: Atlantis
Temp: 26°C	Time: 51 mins	Depth: 43m	Rated: 4

This time it was just Jenny, a Spanish couple and me, all four of us experienced instructors. What a pleasure. Absolutely beautiful dive; the blue of the sea was extraordinary. This time we deliberately went into deco so we could spend 14 minutes at the bottom. Same beautiful things, but such a sense of awe at being down there, so deep, so clear, so lovely. Long, slow ascent, of course, but it was so worth it.

Dive #: 773	Date: 25th February		Dive Site: Atlantis
Temp: 26°C	Time: 46 mins	Depth: 43m	Rated: 5

Again just the four of us. I had fun riding on the tractor down to the beach. Again the deep, deep blue with the sparkle of white bubbles rising. Just lovely being at 43m and still looking at the reef, clearing my mask, completely relaxed.

This time, as we reached 14 minutes, our planned ascent time, we saw the black nudi that Jenny has identified, the first ever new ID for Mozambique. Not only that, but it was next to a beautiful orange-and-purple Spanish dancer. Result was that we only ascended at 17 minutes, so although Rupert had reset my Suunto to have a partial pressure of 1.6 I still had 11 minutes deco to do at 10m, while the others on their Aladdins had 6 minutes. Never mind; beautiful hanging there in the blue and no one minded hanging out with me. The sort of dive nobody wants to end.

Gozo Azul (Blue Fun)

DIVE CENTRE

- Good rental equipment
- Hot and cold showers, toilet
- Free tea and coffee
- Reference books, comfortable relaxation area
- Staff help prepare for dive

DIVES

Single or double tank: Usually return between dives, but will do double tanks on request

Divers per group: Average of nine, with max 14

DMs per group: One or two, depending on group size and ability

Centre to launch: About 6 mins on a custom-built tractor trailer

Boatride to dive sites: 5–25 mins

Dive policy: Buddy pairs stay together; DM must be able to see all divers at all times

End of dive policy: 50-bar rule per diver on shallow dives; divers come up as a group on deep dives.

Main attractions: Marine life and topography; one of their dive sites, The Pinnacle, is considered to be among the top 10 shark-diving sites in the world.

Yellow leaf fish *Taenianotus triacanthus*

Bluespotted ribbontail ray *Taeniura lymma*

Dive centre

BOATS

🐾 2 x 8m rubber ducks with 2 x Suzuki
90/115 h.p. 4-stroke engines
🐾 Equipped with the latest depth sounder,
GPS and safety equipment
🐾 Oxygen on all dive trips

ACCOMMODATION

Gozo offers a variety of options to suit
different budgets and preferences.

GENERAL

Comprises: Dive centre and various options
for accommodation
Website: www.gozo-azul.co.za
Email: natalie@gozo-azul.co.za
Nearest airport: Maputo or Durban
Operating since: 2006
Courses offered: PADI

Golden kingfish *Gnathanodon speciosus*

Nudibranch *Caloria indica*

WHAT THEY SAY

Our staff is professional, experienced and dedicated. We offer personalised service with luxury and comfort and will go the extra mile.

WHAT WE SAY

Exceptional place. The owners, Natalie and Marcus, go out of their way to make sure everyone has exactly the experience they are looking for. They manage to balance safety and professionalism with a relaxed and friendly atmosphere. Everything is well organised and prepared ahead of time, so that each diver can relax and just enjoy the diving.

EXTRACTS FROM ROBYNN'S DIVE LOG

Dive #: 757 **Date:** 7th February **Dive Site:** Doodles
Temp: 26°C **Time:** 57 mins **Depth:** 17m **Rated:** 4

A really lovely dive. Masses of highly colourful fish, two very big groupers, the biggest guitarfish I've ever seen and big and small stingrays. Was lying on the sand trying to look inside in a cave when I heard the guy next to me call out. A very big grouper had bumped into him. He moved away and the grouper nudged my face gently, so I nudged back. It stayed with me for quite a while — so friendly and curious.

Dive #: 766 **Date:** 18th February **Dive Site:** Creche
Temp: 26°C **Time:** 55 mins **Depth:** 16m **Rated:** 3

Very pretty, with lots of highly coloured juveniles. Warm blue water with reasonable vis.

Dive #: 770 **Date:** 23rd February **Dive Site:** Atlantis
Temp: 26°C **Time:** 51 mins **Depth:** 46m **Rated:** 5

Fabulous dive. Two large Spanish dancers with different coloration. Then my first sea apple. Wonderful to be so deep; couldn't resist going a bit deeper than everyone else and touching the sand at 46m.

After 11 minutes at the bottom we made a long, slow ascent. Grey reef shark, a graciously gliding devil ray that stayed with us for ages, and then two devil rays almost touching my fins. Lovely, lovely.

Grey reef shark

Dennis King

Dolphin Encountours Research Center

DOLPHIN ENCOUNTOURS RESEARCH CENTER

Not strictly a dive centre, but rather a group that takes people on dolphin swims.

THE SWIMS

How long? Each trip lasts about two hours.
How many? Between six and 12 per trip
Who is in charge? All trips are led by the owner, Angie Gullan, or a dolphin swim facilitator trained by her.
When should we go? One can see dolphins year-round and whales in winter. Dolphin swims are good all year, but the quality of encounters is better if you can avoid peak season (South African school holidays).

BOAT

1 x 8m semi-rigid rubber duck

Indian Ocean bottlenose dolphin *Tursiops aduncus* and a whale shark *Rhinocodon typus*

Angie knows each one of these wild dolphins by name.

A family of Indian Ocean bottlenose dolphins playing in the breaking waves just off Ponta

The wild dolphins often swim close to snorkellers.

ACCOMMODATION

Angie knows all the facilities in the area well and will help you to find the perfect accommodation to suit your needs.

GENERAL

Comprises: Dolphin swim centre
Website: www.dolphincenter.org and
www.dolphincare.org
Email: angie@dolphincare.org
Nearest airport: Maputo
Operating since: 1995
Owner/manager: Angie Gullan

WHAT THEY SAY

We share a 21-year relationship with these dolphins. Our work supports research, conservation and the long-term monitoring of the dolphins in Ponta.

Note that pre-booking is required. Prior to arrival, participants receive information about what to bring and how to prepare for the open-ocean experience with wild dolphins. Guests meet at the centre at the appointed time, where they are shown how to swim with dolphins and are then taken down to the launch site on the beach.

WHAT WE SAY

This centre really offers the experience of a lifetime. Because Angie has been swimming with these dolphins for the past 21 years, she knows each one personally. They come to her when they see her in the water and clearly enjoy interacting with her. If you are lucky enough to be near her in the water you may experience this privilege too.

Dolphin Encountours Research Center

Angie swimming with a dolphin named Rocha

Scuba Adventures

DIVE CENTRE

🐾 Spacious kit-up area virtually on the beach, at the resort

🐾 Outdoor hot showers and ablution block

🐾 The adjacent reasonably priced restaurant opens an hour before the first launch for pre-dive coffee or breakfast.

DIVES

Single or double tank: Usually return between dives, but will do double tanks on request

Divers per group: Average 4–14

DMs per group: One or two depending on group size and certification standards

Centre to launch: A short ride on a custom tractor-trailer

Boat ride to dive sites: 15–45 mins

Dive policy: Buddy pairs must stay together; DM must be able to see all divers at all times.

End of dive policy: At 50 bars, divers notify DM and ascend up the buoyline with buddies

BOATS

🐾 3 x 8.5m customised semi-rigid inflatables

🐾 Oxygen on all boats

ACCOMMODATION

Self-camping, safari tents, casitas or en-suite beach units available on the beach. Restaurant and self-catering communal kitchen with fridges, braai and cooking facilities, pots, pans, tables, chairs and washing-up facilities.

Beachfront chalet with sea view

The dive boats launch very close to the beach huts.

The loggerhead *Caretta caretta* is southern Africa's most common turtle species.

GENERAL

Comprises: Dive centre, dive charters and accommodation

Websites: www.moz.travel, www.scubaadventures.co.za, www.pontabeachcamps.co.za

Email: info@moz.travel

Nearest airport: Maputo

Operating since: 1997

Courses offered: PADI courses offered in English and Portuguese

WHAT THEY SAY

We are a PADI five-star resort and the longest established dive operation in Mozambique. We provide professional, affordable dive packages. Our 'Half Price Buddy' deals are legendary among divers, as are our affordable accommodation and meal packages. We were awarded 'Best Establishment and Best Value for Money in Ponta do Ouro 2015' by Sleeping Out, based on their readers' reviews.

WHAT WE SAY

Great location and good variety of accommodation options. We stayed in a cabin right on the beach. Very basic but comfortable, with en-suite bathroom (hot shower and loo), good beds, good space for clothes and fabulous views of the sea. We enjoyed sitting on the little stoep and watching the waves roll in.

In addition to the restaurant, there is a communal lapa kitchen with fridges, braai and cooking facilities, wash-up basins and tables. Bring your own cutlery and crockery.

DIVE SITE INFORMATION

Please note that we have not yet dived with Scuba Adventures.

The Whaler –
Underwater Explorer

DIVE CENTRE

- On the beach
- Tea and coffee available
- Divers set up own gear with help from staff
- Fish and coral reference books available
- Hot showers
- No nitrox

DIVES

Single or double tank: Usually return between dives, but do double tanks on request
Divers per group: Max 12
DMs per group: One
Centre to launch: A few mins' walk along the beach

Giant spotted hermit crab *Dardanus megistos*

©www.smishyfish.co.za 2017

The dive centre is right on the beach.

Sunrise over Ponta beach. Another day's dive adventure awaits.

Boat ride to dive sites: About 10 mins
End of dive policy: Buddy pairs go up together
at 50 bar
Main attractions: Lots of varied fish and corals,
including plenty of macro life

BOATS

🐾 2 x dive boats with Yamaha 85h.p. motors
🐾 Oxygen on all boats

ACCOMMODATION

Simple reed huts on the beach. Communal
kitchen. Families welcome.

GENERAL

Consists of: Dive centre and accommodation
Website: www.thewhaler.co.za
Email: mike@thewhaler.co.za,
hilton@thewhaler.co.za
Nearest airport: Maputo
Operating since: 2010
Courses offered: PADI and NAUI (National
Association of Underwater Instructors)

WHAT THEY SAY

We are located right on the beach and offer a
peaceful, relaxed environment.

WHAT WE SAY

This resort is right on the beach. It is spacious
and well organised, with everything you need.
The atmosphere is very laid-back.

Seawhip goby *Bryaninops yongei* on a black coral

Indian Ocean bottlenose dolphins *Tursiops aduncus* enjoying the waves

©www.smishyfish.co.za 2017

Peacock mantis shrimp *Odontodactylus scyllarus*

Blackflap blenny *Cirripectes auritus*

EXTRACTS FROM ROBYNN'S DIVE LOG

| **Dive #:** 759 | **Date:** 9th February | | **Dive Site:** Blacks |
| **Temp:** 27°C | **Time:** 52 mins | **Depth:** 16m | **Rated:** 3 |

Tiny reef but plenty to see. Saw my first ghost pipefish. Delicate and lovely. Two big blue-and-yellow boxfish and one exquisite, tiny, orangey geometric one. Got close to two honeycomb morays.

| **Dive #:** 760 | **Date:** 10th February | | **Dive Site:** Pinnacles |
| **Temp:** 24–27°C | **Time:** 52 mins | **Depth:** 42.7m | **Rated:** 4 |

A different kind of dive. We dropped straight down to 42.7m. Dark and cold at the bottom, we immediately started looking around and easing upward. Nothing unusual to see until we reached about 18m when we saw a beautiful sleek bullshark swimming towards us. He kept coming back. We hung out in the deep blue for about 50 minutes altogether; was really quite magical.

Multicoloured soft corals on the unspoilt reefs off Ponta

Oceana Diving

DIVE CENTRE

🐾 Situated in the peaceful surroundings of Motel do Mar, overlooking the beach of Ponta do Ouro and about 800m from the launch site along the beach

🐾 Tea, coffee and water freely available

DIVES

Single or double tank: Usually return between dives, but will do double tanks on request

Divers per group: Preferred limit of 12, but can take up to 16

DMs per group: One

Centre to launch: Walk to the beach

Boat ride to dive sites: 5–30 mins

Dive policy: Dive as a group

End of dive policy: Usually 60 mins for shallow dives

Main attractions: Densely populated tropical fish and shark dives. Nudibranchs galore, electric blue sea cucumbers, Spanish dancers, goldies, rockcod, chocolate dips, dominos, kingfish and big schools of powder-blue surgeonfish. Pristine coral reefs with beautiful topography.

BOATS

🐾 2 x semi-rigid inflatable dive boats

🐾 DAN oxygen kit on all trips

ACCOMMODATION

Oceana has arrangements with various resorts, and Sandy Probert, the owner, who has lived in the area for many years, will help you find the one that best suits your accommodation needs.

GENERAL

Consists of: Dive centre and dive school

Website: www.pontainfo.com/oceana.html

Email: sandels@cosmiclink.co.za, oceanadiving@cosmiclink.co.za, oceana@pontainfo.com

Nearest airport: Maputo

Operating since: 2006

Courses offered: PADI; Sandy is a PADI MSDT Instructor.

The sea apple *Pseudocolochirus unica* has tentacles around its mouth.

Spanish dancer *Hexabranchus sanguineus*

WHAT THEY SAY

Oceana is an owner-managed dive centre offering friendly personalised service customised to the type of diving you are looking for.

WHAT WE SAY

Being close to the launch site is always good. Sandy is one of the most highly trained medics in Ponta. We know from personal experience that she goes out of her way to take expert care of you in the event of an injury – very comforting when you are far from home.

DIVE SITE INFORMATION

The following are some of Oceana's best dive sites.

Three Sisters

Depth: 24m
Diver level: Advanced
Highlights/Nature of dive: This reef consists of three rocks about 70m apart. This site is very popular because there is a 3m wall along its eastern edge, flattening out to the west. The Main Sister is the biggest rock. To the north of it you will find garden eels on the sand, and may spot an elusive rockmover wrasse flitting between the eels. The fish life consists largely of goldies, rockcod, chocolate dips, dominos, kingfish and big schools of powder-blue surgeonfish. The unspoilt hard and soft corals here are home to porcelain crabs and to carpet anemones, frequented by eggshell shrimps. The

black coral is home to the longnose hawkfish, and not too far away a careful search may reveal the elusive painted frogfish. Often you will find honeycomb moray eels in crevices on the reef. There are nudibranchs galore. This is a great site for all types of photography.

Atlantis

Depth: Varies from 42m on top of the reef to 56m on the sand
Diver level: Advanced divers with deep training
Highlights/Nature of dive: This deep reef reminds one of a sunken city, with huge square boulders like blocks. Whip corals grow between the crevices. Schools of small fish frequent the beautiful green coral trees. Home to electric blue sea cucumbers and Spanish dancers, this reef provides excellent photographic opportunities. In the mid-water you will occasionally see marlin, sharks and sailfish.

Anchor

Depth: 22m
Diver level: Advanced
Highlights/Nature of dive: Not only will you see old anchors on the southern end of the reef, but also two parallel ledges with a variety of reef fish, such as royal angelfish (unique to this site), trumpetfish, longmouth flutefish, butterflyfish, damselfish, anemonefish, eels, crabs, nudibranchs, flatworms, feather stars and starfish. There are beautifully coloured soft corals and anemones, as well as hard corals like staghorn coral. Occasionally you might see a resident grey reef shark.

Popeyed scorpionfish *Rhinopias eschmeyeri*

Gala-Gala Eco Resort & Diving

DIVE CENTRE

- Good rental equipment
- Showers, tea and coffee available
- Reference books and a comfortable area in which to relax
- Conveniently located at the resort

DIVES

Single or double tank: Usually return between dives, but will do double tanks on request

Divers per group: Average 6–8, but will launch for two divers; max 13

DMs per group: Depends on group size and qualifications, but 1–3

Centre to launch: 1km in a 4x4

Boat ride to dive sites: 5–25 mins

Dive policy: DM must be able to see all divers at all times

End of dive policy: 50 bar or 50 mins

Main attractions: Sharks (10 species), friendly potato bass, giant honeycomb eels, ribbon eels, mantas, whales, nudibranchs and big schools of colourful fish. Also cleaning stations, walls, drift dives, swim-throughs and the world-renowned Pinnacles shark dive.

BOATS

- 1 x 8m Superduck with 2 x 90 h.p. Suzuki 4-stroke engines (so no fumes)
- Oxygen on all launches

Zambezi sharks (bull sharks) *Carcharhinus leucas* on the hunt

A yellow-edge moray *Gymnothorax flavimarginatus* shows its backward-facing teeth.

ACCOMMODATION

Quiet and relaxing, the eco resort is set on the village outskirts. It has a comfortable, barefoot luxury, bush-and-beach atmosphere and offers different types of accommodation, including catered and self-catering options. There is a private bar, café and splash pool. No music is allowed; there are no TVs, and noise is discouraged after 22h00.

GENERAL

Comprises: Dive centre and eco resort
Website: www.gala-gala.co.za
Email: bev@gala-gala.co.za
Nearest airport: Maputo; then two hours to Ponta by local or private taxi
Operating since: 2008
Manager: bev@gala-gala.co.za
Courses offered: NAUI, PADI

The cabanas have lovely homely touches.

Comfort and style in an eco-friendly setting

WHAT THEY SAY

We are outside the village in a quiet area. The resort and dive charter are both owner-operated. Having the owners always present ensures a top-quality experience. Dives are mostly DM'ed by the owner. We provide border transfers and other transport if required. Visitors may cater for themselves, or visit the on-site café and bar.

WHAT WE SAY

A uniquely fabulous place if you want somewhere quiet in Ponta. The eco resort is peaceful and natural with every luxury on offer. The dive resort is very professional, with personalised options that bigger centres can't always offer. This is a superb combination of first-class diving and tranquil accommodation.

EXTRACTS FROM ROBYNN'S DIVE LOG

| **Dive #:** 767 | **Date:** 19th February | | **Dive Site:** Atlantis |
| **Temp:** 26°C | **Time:** 51 mins | **Depth:** 37m | **Rated:** 4 |

Absolutely loved this dive, which was run just for me. We dropped into that incredible blue and sank slowly. After spending 11 minutes at 36m we slowly ascended for the rest of the dive, looking out for 'big stuff', which never came. The highlight was seeing two devil rays glide slowly past. So tranquil, blue and warm!

| **Dive #:** 768 | **Date:** 20th February | | **Dive Site:** Pinnacles |
| **Temp:** 26–27°C | **Time:** 51 mins | **Depth:** 36.7m | **Rated:** 4 |

Again the deep blue, with warm water. Utterly lovely. And out of the blue came three hammerheads. More than I've ever seen together in my life before. They came and went a few times: amazingly sensitive and evolved, they are always fascinating. Then a blacktip circled round about three times, in hunting mode.

| **Dive #:** 769 | **Date:** 21st February 2015 | | **Dive Site:** Pinnacles |
| **Temp:** 26°C | **Time:** 50 mins | **Depth:** 36.7m | **Rated:** 4 |

I was lucky to be invited on this dive with a French film crew making a film about the relationship between dolphins and humans. They wanted shark footage, hence Pinnacles. Once again the deep, endless blue, with the sparkle of the bubbles rising up. Two minutes into the dive we saw a grey reef shark. Then the three hammerheads from yesterday approached, seeming interested in

Scalloped hammerhead

Dennis King

us. They came past time and again, as did some solo hammerheads. Near the end, a silvertip shark darted past, then came straight for me but turned at the last minute. So enchanting, the whole thing. The cameramen said they didn't get useful footage because the sharks didn't come close enough and there were particles in the water affecting the light.

Justin Barker

A curious green turtle *Chelonia mydas* joins the dive.

Many divers find that their place of
greatest contentment is underwater.
Photo: Daniel van Duinkerken

Appendix –
Health and safety

D iving in Mozambique is of the first order, and many of the dive resorts are on par with the best in the world, but it must always be borne in mind that you will be travelling in Africa. Mozambique is one of the world's poorest countries, with very limited services and resources, and dive resorts are often in very remote areas. For this reason, it is important to exercise good judgement in staying healthy and avoiding injury. This section should assist you in your preparations, but should not replace consulting with a knowledgeable dive/travel physician.

As mentioned in the summary on p.10, most divers travelling to exotic destinations worry about rare problems like decompression sickness, envenomation by marine creatures like stonefish, and dread diseases when, in fact, you are far more likely to experience a bout of traveller's diarrhoea, sunburn or an ear infection, any of which could ruin your dive holiday. For all of these conditions prevention is better than cure.

Touching a stonefish *Synanceia verrucosa* can result in hours of pain or even death.

GENERAL CONSIDERATIONS
Health services in Mozambique
More than 60 per cent of Mozambique's population lives in rural areas with little or no access to health services. A network of health posts and clinics feeds into a few regional hospitals. There are only about three doctors per 100,000 people across the country. Therefore, publically accessible health services are often very rudimentary, and it is important to have made independent plans to acquire high-quality care in the case of an emergency. This usually requires suitable pre-planning and the purchase of health and evacuation insurance. (See p.159.) Fortunately, this is generally quite cost-effective.

Avoiding common illnesses
You can expect your body to take some time to adjust to a new environment, particularly if coming from abroad. Jet lag is common, and can be reduced by setting your watch to the Mozambique time-zone when you board your flight, getting some exercise before bed when you land, and allowing yourself some time to adjust before starting to dive. Gastrointestinal upsets are common, and can vary from simple traveller's diarrhoea

Setting up dive gear is a serious business requiring systematic checks that could save the diver's life.

Nuarro Lodge

An injury from a long-spined urchin *Diadema setosum* can be very painful.

to more serious infections. The use of strict hand-washing practices, caution in using local water sources, good personal hygiene and probiotics (or natural culture yoghurt) will reduce the risks. Sunburn is unpleasant at best and debilitating at worst, but is completely preventable with appropriate attire and the liberal use of sunscreen. Remember, if you are not used to the African sun, you will burn easily. Don't forget sunglasses with UV protection to wear on the beach and the boat – solar keratitis (sunburn of the cornea of the eye, akin to snow-blindness) will ruin your trip and prevent you from diving.

A problem that is particular to diving, especially in the tropics, is the development of ear canal infections (called *otitis externa*, or 'swimmer's ear'). This happens with frequent dives in areas with high humidity, where the ear canal remains warm and moist, allowing bacteria to proliferate. This is best prevented by carefully rinsing and drying the ears after each dive; alcohol-containing eardrops are very useful. If you have suffered from this condition previously, or are undertaking a long trip, it may be worth taking some antibiotic- and steroid-containing eardrops.

Malaria

Malaria, which is endemic in Mozambique, is a parasitic disease carried by mosquitoes. It remains the deadliest disease in Africa. All areas of Mozambique (and all the diving regions described in this book) are considered high risk for malaria. Many misconceptions exist regarding malaria in travellers. For instance, some people believe that prophylaxis can hide infection (it can), and because malaria is easy to treat (it generally is), it is better to forgo preventative medicines and simply deal with the infection if it occurs. This is dangerous and inadvisable. While most cases of malaria are easily treated with modern drugs, it still is responsible for many deaths and lasting disability (such as recurrent cerebral malaria), even in healthy travellers. Prophylaxis and measures to prevent being bitten by mosquitoes are thus always recommended. Measures to avoid being bitten include covering exposed skin (with long sleeves and trousers) or moving indoors during the dawn and dusk hours, using insect repellent, mosquito screens and nets.

It is worthwhile to consult a travel doctor or clinic for advice before your trip, but the information below may be useful. Around 90 per cent of the malaria in Mozambique is of the *Plasmodium falciparum* subtype, to which (at the time of writing) there is local resistance to chloroquine. The US Centers for Disease Control (CDC, **www.cdc.gov**) maintains an excellent resource on the current recommendations for anti-malaria prophylaxis, which currently include atovaquone-proguanil, doxycycline and mefloquine (although mefloquine is not recommended for divers). When obtaining prescriptions for prophylaxis, make sure to mention that you are diving. Some more in-depth information about the specific medications can be found in the box on p.156.

MALARIA PROPHYLAXIS AND DIVING

There is no specific evidence on the safety of scuba diving while using antimalarial drugs. Despite this, there are some practical considerations, and most diving doctors recommend against the use of mefloquine, because of side effects that mimic decompression illness and may impair divers. Note that the prevalence of malaria and resistance to various drugs varies around the world. The advice below is specific to Mozambique. Information may change over time, and the reader is encouraged to check a resource such as the Centers for Disease Control (**www.cdc.gov**) before travelling to confirm if any new information has emerged.

Malaria prophylaxis that is considered safe for divers

❑ Doxycycline (Doximal®/Vibramycin®/Cyclidox®/etc): One of the most reliable prophylactic drugs (99 per cent effective), and the most commonly recommended drug in areas with resistant malaria, such as Mozambique. It also offers some protection against tick-bite fever (Rickettsia) and cholera, and at higher doses can be used to treat other bacterial and protozoal infections. It is thus very useful to have it with you. Daily dose is 100mg in adults, for up to eight weeks' duration. It is also usually the cheapest of the prophylactic drugs. The downsides are that it must be continued for four weeks after return, and its side-effect profile includes nausea, particularly if taken on an empty stomach, vomiting, diarrhoea, sun sensitivity and allergic responses. It also decreases the efficacy of oral contraceptives. Unsafe in pregnancy (as is diving). Not safe for breastfeeding or for children under eight years of age. The Divers Alert Network (DAN) recommends doxycycline as their first choice for prophylaxis in chloroquine-resistant areas.

❑ Atorvaquone & proguanil (Malarone®/Mozitec®): Convenient dosing; needs to be continued for only seven days after leaving the malaria area. It is the newest and, currently, most expensive drug. Originally considered inadvisable for divers, the consensus has shifted and it is now being recommended more frequently.

❑ Chloroquine: Generally considered safe for diving. It is safe in pregnancy, but there is widespread resistance to chloroquine in Mozambique, and it is therefore not recommended.

❑ Chloroquine & proguanil: Considered safe for diving; safe in pregnancy if folate supplementation is used. DAN second choice in resistant areas. Must be used for four weeks after return. Proguanil cannot be used without chloroquine.

Malaria prophylaxis to be avoided by divers:

❑ Mefloquine (Lariam®/Mefliam®): Usually not recommended for divers because of side effects that include loss of fine motor co-ordination, vertigo and drowsiness, and that can mimic the symptoms of decompression sickness. Suitable for non-diving travellers; convenient once-weekly dose of 250mg orally in adults. Considered safe in pregnancy after the first trimester, and during breastfeeding for babies over 5kg.

❑ Arthemeter (Cotexin®), quinine, sulphadoxine & pyrimethaminse (Fansidar®) and halofantrine (Halfan®) are used in treatment or are outmoded prophylactics, and are not recommended for malaria prevention.

Other infections

In addition to malaria, there are other infectious diseases to be aware of, such as hepatitis, typhoid, rabies, and HIV. You should consult your travel doctor about these concerns, depending on your risk profile. Routine (normal) immunisations as per your home country (such as measles/ mumps/rubella, diphtheria, varicella, polio and influenza) should be up to date. Yellow fever is *not* found in Mozambique, and you only need immunisation (and proof thereof) if you are travelling to Mozambique from any country where it is endemic. Recently, Zika virus has become established in the region. While this is of little threat to adults and the risk of infection is low, pregnant women should carefully consider the risk of travel to the area.

Dangerous animals

Although snakebite is a common fear and there are numerous poisonous species in the region, it is a very rare event (much like shark attacks) and almost never occurs when treating wildlife with respect. If you see a snake (or shark!), observe its beauty from a safe distance, and do not engage in any threatening or provoking behaviour. Large game and predators do exist in the wilderness areas, but you will be highly unlikely to encounter them on a diving trip.

MEDICAL CONSIDERATIONS FOR SCUBA DIVING

Fitness for diving

Diving is a relaxed sport, but it does require a modicum of fitness and that any chronic illnesses be well controlled. In particular, many dives in Mozambique can feature strong currents. Good buoyancy control and being fit enough to kick hard for short distances are important. If you have any medical conditions, or become short of breath on moderate exertion, it is advisable to see your doctor

well before the trip. If any doubt exists, a qualified dive physician should be consulted.

All divers would avoid a dive when they have a cold or flu under normal circumstances, but when on a holiday they have planned for months, will often take a chance. Don't forget that a cold can lead to severe and even debilitating sinus squeeze or reverse block underwater – it's not worth the risk. If you develop a cold, enjoy the African sun above the water until it is fully resolved.

Diving and pregnancy

Diving at any time during pregnancy is not recommended. If pregnancy is suspected (or even possible), or for women not using regular contraception, it is worthwhile to take a simple pregnancy test before departing on a scuba diving holiday. This is also important in Mozambique, as some antimalarial medications are not safe in pregnancy (see opposite).

Seasickness

Wisdom has it that there are three phases to seasickness: when you are scared that you are going to get sick, when you are so sick that you are scared you will die, and when you are so sick you're scared you won't die. None of these is conducive to having a great dive. If you know that you suffer from motion sickness, it is worthwhile taking some preventative medicine with you. Fortunately, many options exist, although they all have potential side-effects. Commonly recommended agents include cinnarizine (Stugeron®), hyoscine butylbromide/hydrobromide (Scopoderm®/ Buscopan®), prochloroperazine (Stemetil®), ondansetron (Zofran®) or dimenhydremate (Dizinil®). Side effects of these medications include many conditions that may make diving unsafe, such as blurred vision, drowsiness and confusion. Therefore, it is strongly recommended that each individual tries the medication in question before the trip to test for any adverse effects. Most people can find a drug that works for them. Recently, more attention has turned to the use of phenytoin (Dilantin®), an anti-epileptic medication that has been shown to be very effective in preventing motion sickness. Although it is not without the potential for side effects, it appears to be very safe, but it requires a prescription and few doctors are aware of this use.

Marine envenomation

Like any marine environment, Mozambican waters contain various creatures that can deliver venom through a bite or sting. Fortunately, most are avoidable. Bites from sea snakes are so rare as not to warrant discussion. Stingrays, stonefish, lionfish and other vertebrate stings are immediately excruciatingly painful (and occasionally lethal), but their protein-based poison is inactivated by hot water. (Think hot bath, not boiling kettle). Jellyfish stings are fairly common, but there are no known species that are regarded as life-threatening to a healthy adult human. Unfortunately, this doesn't make the stings any more pleasant. A Lycra® or neoprene exposure suit will offer good protection. If you are stung, treatment is determined by the offending

©www.smishyfish.co.za 2017

Portuguese Man O'War or bluebottle
Physalia physalis

species: the Portuguese Man O'War requires hot water, while box jellyfish require an acidic solution such as vinegar. Liberal washing with clean water will be helpful in all cases. Do not use solutions such as alcohol or suntan lotion.

Flying after diving

Don't forget that although most passenger aircraft are pressurised, the cabin pressure is still much lower than at sea level, and decompression sickness can occur if you fly too soon after diving. The generally accepted guidelines are for a minimum of 12 hours after a single dive, or 24 hours after performing multiple or deep dives. This includes single dives over successive days. (Some consider 18 hours sufficient). When making your travel plans, remember to allow a full day between your last dive and your flight home, and then stick to this plan. This is often a good time to book a non-diving activity in the local area, to help you avoid the temptation to do just one more dive!

DIVING MEDICAL EMERGENCIES

Safe diving practices

Remember that you are in a remote location with limited support. Conservative diving practices with safe profiles, modest bottom times and mandatory safety stops are advised for all dives. While it is ideal for every diver to have a dive computer, taking along (and knowing how to use) dive tables will help if the batteries go flat. Plan the deepest dive of the day as the first dive, and allow generous surface intervals.

Dealing with emergencies

Medical emergencies that occur during diving are usually caused by adverse pressure effects during rapid ascent (dysbarism or barotrauma) or the formation of nitrogen bubbles in the tissues (decompression sickness, DCS). Both can be avoided by safe diving practices, but when they occur, require rapid intervention to prevent further injury or death. Any acute symptoms on surfacing from a dive should be considered to be dive-related until proven otherwise. Typical symptoms of decompression sickness include:

- limb or joint pain, tingling or 'pins and needles'
- chest, stomach or back pain
- muscle weakness, often in the legs
- loss of balance
- general weakness
- visual disturbances and confusion
- mottled or spotty red skin rash
- difficulty breathing or breathlessness
- coughing and pink frothy sputum

In all cases, the same basic treatment applies:

- The victim should be reassured, allowed to lie down, kept calm, and kept warm.
- If available, oxygen should be given with a snug mask or demand valve.
- In-water recompression should not be attempted unless expert assistance is available.
- The emergency plan should be implemented and the victim transferred as rapidly as possible to a dive doctor and recompression chamber.
- Gather as much useful information as possible, including: dive history and profile (max depth, duration, safety and decompression stops of all recent dives, history of rapid ascent), time of surfacing, time of onset of symptoms, underlying medical conditions, treatment steps undertaken, medical insurance information, etc.
- Don't forget to check the diver's buddy, who is equally at risk!

Recompression chamber facilities in Mozambique

At the time of writing, there are no recompression chamber facilities in reliable operation in Mozambique. Fortunately, health-care and chamber facilities in neighbouring South Africa are of a very high standard. Evacuation by air to a chamber in Durban (or even Cape Town) can be achieved within a matter of a few hours if logistic and insurance arrangements are in place. There are no medical helicopter services available in Mozambique, although private aircraft (such as resort-owned helicopters) may be used to assist. In the very far south (Ponto do Ouro and surrounds), it may be feasible to move the patient overland to the border, and airlift to Richards Bay from there. In other areas, an air ambulance will have to be dispatched, which will incur delays with customs and immigration. It is strongly recommended to have specific insurance cover, or membership of an organisation such as the Divers Alert Network, who are well versed in dealing with these challenges (see below).

Travel and medical insurance

Many travellers will have some degree of automatic cover if they have bought their travel tickets using a credit card or by notifying their medical insurers of their travel plans. However, it is important to read the details of these free policies carefully, as they often explicitly exclude adventure activities such as scuba diving. In the event of an emergency (especially if it requires evacuation or repatriation for treatment), it is valuable to have peace of mind, knowing that you are covered for these costs. Readily available proof of insurance will also speed up these processes and prevent delays while you assemble proof of your ability to pay for the services.

Often, it is quite cost-effective to obtain simple 'top-up' cover on your automatic travel insurance policy, which will then cover adventure activities and have greater funds available for evacuation and treatment. The best way to do this is to contact the insurance agents directly and tell them explicitly where you plan to go and what you plan to do (including scuba diving) and ask what policy is required. This can often be done telephonically.

Another good option for travel, medical and dive-related insurance is to become a member of the Divers Alert Network (DAN), or to purchase a single-trip policy from them. This has the added advantage of giving you access to good advice specifically for divers, up-to-date information regarding services such as recompression chambers, and 24-hour telephonic access to qualified diving doctors.

It is well worthwhile to have a physical copy of all insurance details, contact information, background medical information and the passport of each member of your group stored in an easily accessible location (such as in the group leader or buddy's luggage) for use in case of an emergency.

FURTHER INFORMATION

Contact the author for advice and assistance: ross@wildmedix.com
Diver's Alert Network (DAN): www.diversalertnetwork.org/
DAN Southern Africa: www.dansa.org/malaria.htm
DAN contact numbers in Africa: +27 828 106 010 (or 0800 020 111 in South Africa)
DAN advice on malaria and diving: www.dive-the-world.com/newsletter-200503-malaria-and-diving.php
London Diving Chamber: A resource for diving emergencies, run by divers for divers. See http://londondivingchamber.co.uk/ or contact the hotline on +447940 353 816

A geometric moray *Gymnothorax griseus* rests among sea grass.